STEVEN PAUL DAVIES

ALEX COX

FILM ANARCHIST

A catalogue record for this book is available from the British Library.

ISBN 0 7134 8670 8

Printed in England by
Butler and Tanner, Frome, Somerset

Designed by Simon Rosenheim

First published in 2000 by
B T Batsford
9 Blenheim Court
Brewery Road
London N7 9NT

A member of the Chrysalis Group plc

Contents

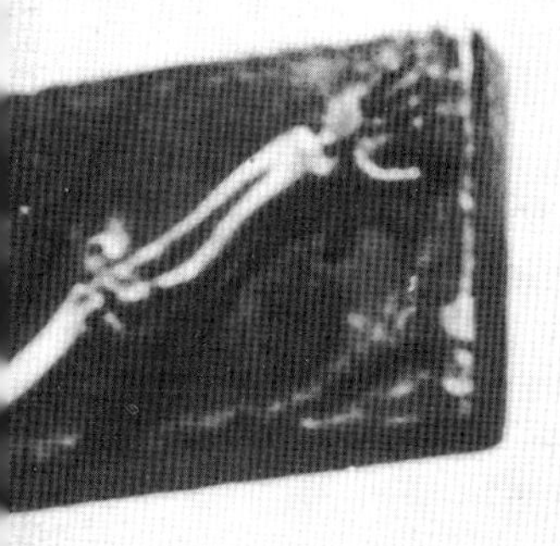

Acknowledgements

Principal thanks go to Alex Cox for his willingness to talk about his life and work. Special thanks to Tod Davies; for use of photos, Peter McCarthy, Martin Turner (for the photos from *Repo Man*), Katsumi Ishikuma and Kuniaki Negishi; Christopher Eccleston; Eric Fellner; Nick Jones; David Hayman; Miguel Sandoval; Peter Boyle; Dan Wool; Abbe Wool; Zander Schloss; Rudy Wurlitzer; Gavin Smith at Film Comment magazine and to Dennis Hopper for his kind interest and support.

Cover photograph by Shinichi Yokoyama.

Foreword

My first meeting with Alex Cox was over a stale hot dog on the sunset strip. A tall, red-headed, lanky drink of water with a Liverpool accent. He was a student at UCLA having received a Fullbright fellowship. He had a film he wanted to make called *Repo Man*. It was 1983. He wanted me to play in it; I liked the part. It was an uneventful meeting, and I decided that they probably wouldn't get financing. Harry Dean Stanton played the part – it was a good, solid first film with a touch of surrealism, and was financially successful. Then I saw *Sid & Nancy* or *Love Kills*. It was an amazing film – a winner for all time. *Sid & Nancy* is a film that deals with a period of time and space that no other film has dealt with – a brilliant emotional experience. S&M, drugs, punk, rock'n'roll, assassination of the senses. The film seems to self-destruct with Sid Vicious our protagonist. Brilliant! One of the important films of the century. *Love Kills* or *Sid & Nancy* got Cox into my dream club of directors. In 1987 I wanted to start a company of directors with Alex Cox, David Lynch, Bigas Luna, Wim Wenders, and myself. The dream was short lived because of financing.

Then in '87 I worked for Alex in *Straight to Hell*. I went to Almería, Spain and played opposite Grace Jones. We only worked a day. I played IG Farben. I had a briefcase of automatic weapons. Coincidentally, IG Farben is the same name as the German industrialist who supplied Hitler with his weapons.

Holding court, Alex was omniscient. He had been wildly praised at Cannes for *Love Kills* and deservedly so. So he grabbed the torch, wrote a script in three days, and went on a shooting spree in Spain. *Walker* was taking too long to set up in Mexico, and it looked like he was going to have to go to Nicaragua. When I arrived in Spain for my one day, *Straight to Hell* was like a disorganized rock concert. He told me in a quiet manic moment at lunch that all he was interested in was power. He needed power and

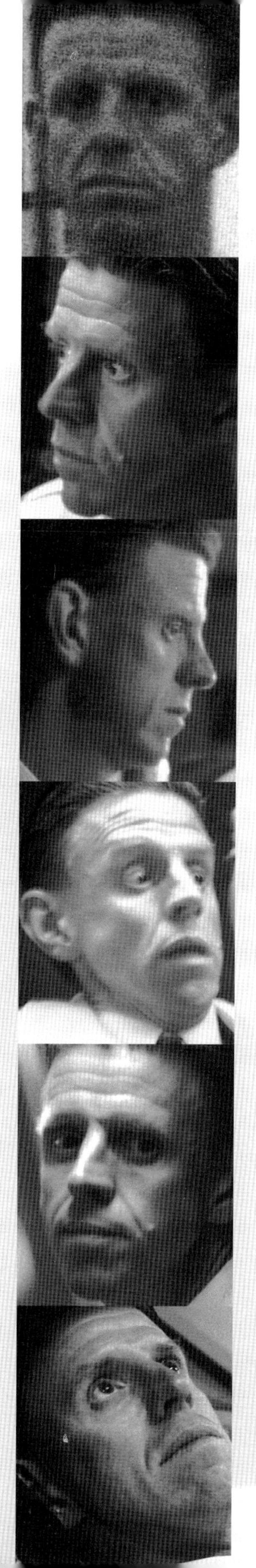

lots of it. We had talked about *Walker* before *Straight to Hell* in Los Angeles. We discussed it again. It had been very difficult for him to get financing and he was off to Nicaragua to film with the blessings of the Sandanista National Liberation Front. Ed Harris was to play Walker.

I told Alex that I thought that, for one day, IG Farben had a lot of dialogue. So I told Alex I would only say the lines when I was facing camera. When my back was to camera, I would only gesture and pretend to be speaking. I would time it so that we could dub in the necessary lines later. At first, he balked at the idea, but then he agreed when he saw me doing it. It worked very well once Grace Jones arrived on the set after five hours in makeup. Grace Jones is a gloriously striking woman. In my opinion she had been even more beautiful before she went into makeup, but I guess for her confidence is everything. We shot the scene with minimal effort. I saw *Straight to Hell* in a private showing for the Vicomte and Vicomtesse de Noailles at the Pic-Wik Drive-In, Studio City, Los Angeles. It was long and slow with flashes of genius. I saw *Walker* and felt the same, although I believe *Walker* a much superior film and historically important. I suppose the same could be said of *Straight to Hell* – a homage to the spaghetti western in a James Joyceian sort of way. I hired Alex and his partner Tod Davies to rewrite *Back Track* [alias *Catch Fire*] and for Alex to play the ghost of DH Lawrence. What a wonderful experience that was. A dedicated, disciplined writer and wonderful actor with beard and accent – a remarkable performance and resemblance to Lawrence.

I saw his *Highway Patrolman*, a masterful little film. I was impressed with the economy of script and the way of shooting. Alex Cox is back on track, not that he had left his track, but a more accessible track – minimal, well-paced film-making – a joy to see.

In a side story, Alex and myself were having lunch in West Beach Café discussing 'The Shining Path' – a leftist revolutionary movement in the mountains of Peru where I had shot *The Last Movie*. During the conversation I told Alex I was a republican. He didn't believe me, so I showed him my republican card congratulating me for having elected the new Senate – whereupon he grabbed it, ripped it in half, and shouted, "You *must* be a working class hero!" I mumbled, "I am, I just don't like big government." I guess he didn't hear me or didn't want to, nor should he. Absolute power is necessary to create. Absolute power corrupts. So keep creating and corrupting – I know you will, and brilliantly.

Your amigo

Dennis Hopper

Chapter One

Introduction

When a true genius appears in the world,
you will know him by this sign,
that the dunces are all in confederacy
against him.

Jonathan Swift

Alex Cox lives life on the edge. He is not totally anti-Hollywood but believes there is something fundamentally wrong with much of mainstream film-making:

> "There is no place in Hollywood for certain directors. It has to do with the big corporation owning the studios and being tied into the military–industrial complex, or the Mafia. The movie business feels it must support war and encourage white yuppies to have babies. If you don't buy into that you are ultimately excluded."

A true maverick director, Cox is one of the few British film-makers of his generation – the younger – to have made his reputation in the US. Injecting a punk sensibility into film-making, he has experienced both mainstream success and cult adulation, not to mention critical acclaim. With films such as *Repo Man* and *Sid and Nancy*, Alex Cox established himself as a highly acclaimed cult auteur. Later, with increasingly experimental films such as *Walker*, *El Patrullero* and *Death and the Compass*, he maintained this originality and quality and sought to break away from traditional cinematic language and narrative. *Alex Cox: Film Anarchist* charts his development as a film-maker but also reveals the obsessions that continue to dominate his increasingly rich and complex body of work.

There is no doubt that Alex Cox has proved himself not only as a film-maker but also as a film critic. As the presenter of the long-running BBC2 series *Moviedrome* for seven years, his original and compelling Sunday night introductions to a variety of classic films were watched by millions. Unlike many critics, Cox's talk was brash and colloquial with a savage directness; a fluid, manic, mercurial style that was free, as opposed to some strained imitation of literature.

This fully authorised biography is the result of Cox's willingness to talk for the first time at length about his life and work and about his major influences. Interviews were conducted over a period of about 12 months, mainly in London and Liverpool and, occasionally, by long distance phone call. I listened to him with a gut admiration as he interpreted his films and the reaction they provoked, including his own reaction to the continued cult status of *Repo Man* and *Sid & Nancy* and how his anarchic black comedy *Straight to Hell* was completely misunderstood. The book also unveils Cox's opinions on the punk scene and subsequent war of words with Johnny Rotten, as well as his troubled tenure as the original director of *Fear and Loathing in Las Vegas* and a crazed encounter with Hunter S. Thompson. Also detailed is Cox's hatred of the Hollywood culture, his appreciation of Mexican cinema and how he became directly involved with this intriguing national film industry.

This is the first biography of Alex Cox and his co-operation also extended to providing the numerous behind-the-scenes stills that appear throughout the book.

Steven Paul Davies

Chapter Two

From Liverpool to LA

What comes into the world and disturbs nothing deserves neither consideration nor patience.

Rene Char

acclaimed film director Alex Cox achieved his first distinction on the day he was born, that of Clatterbridge Hospital's 'Longest Baby' (as opposed to 'Largest Baby'). A cardboard scouser, not a 'real' one because he's from 'over the water', he was born just outside Liverpool on 15th December 1954.

Cox grew up in Bebington. From a solidly middle-class family background, his father worked as an engineer for Burmah Oil in Ellsemere Port and his mother was what he describes as "a professional mother". However, despite what would appear to be a perfectly 'normal' childhood, Cox always sensed he was an outsider. At St Andrews primary school, he realised he was a little bit different:

> "Up until a certain point, we all used to play together, but at the age of about nine, all the boys started chasing a football and I was the only one who remained with the girls. It seemed very odd to the others and made me a bit of an outcast."

His enjoyment at St Andrews soon ended when he started at the single sex Wirral Grammar School or "the prison for children" as Cox describes it. It was where Socialist Prime Minister Harold Wilson was educated and Cox would later follow Wilson to Oxford.

The man later to be responsible for the highly subversive historical epic *Walker* was brought up in a naturally left wing environment. In a time when Britain was a predominantly socialist nation, it was very common to be of the Left. Cox simply found it odd that anyone would be right wing and fetishistic about private property:

> "The State owned everything, so the people owned everything. The revenue of British Telecom and British Airways went to pay for our National Health and our education. I sort of presumed we were always going to have State ownership of everything. Not a Communist world because they were just as insane as the capitalists, but rather some sort of Socialist paradise where we'd all get two weeks at Butlins every year! My beliefs are also in part down to geography. How can you be from the north of England and also be a Tory? You'd have to be insane! I know that there are right wing people up there but there's no money. It's completely poor and backward because all the money is concentrated in the south of England. You have to be rebellious if you're from the north because we're at war with the dominant culture. We grew up at war with the dominant culture so it's natural to remain opposed to the status quo, which, in Britain, is London. What's weird is how everything shifted. All the dialogue is now so right wing."

In 1987 Cox leapt at the chance to attack the right wing status quo. He used the nineteenth-century true story of William Walker seizing Nicaragua by force, to protest against the Reagan administration's proxy war on Nicaragua's democratically elected Sandinista government: "William Walker was an American cut-throat, like an Oliver North-type pirate."

As a teenager Cox spent most of his free time in the cinemas in Liverpool: the ABC, the Odeon, the Scala and the Futurist, as well as two cartoon cinemas called the JC and the Tatler. However, the latter two soon became very dubious soft porn cinemas and later art-house theatres. Eventually, the two buildings were torn down and replaced by shopping centres. Before their demise, during the brief art-house phase, Cox went to see films that had a profound effect on him. At the Tatler he saw

« Philip Franks in Cox's production of Brecht's *The Resistible Rise of Arturo Ui.*

King Kong projected in 35mm. What impressed him as he walked out of the theatre back on to the streets of Liverpool was how much his city had in common with Manhattan:

> "In the centre of Liverpool, the buildings were built on a grand scale. They were blocks long. The city was built to impress the foreigners when they came in on the ocean liners. They would see the Liver building, the Cunard building, the gigantic insurance buildings and they'd stop at the Adelphi Hotel. Liverpool was a big deal at that time. It was like the ghost of New York."

Because his grandfather knew the manager of the ABC, a 14-year-old Cox was allowed to get in to see *The Wild Bunch*, despite it being an X-rated film, and at the Scala, he was chilled by the nihilism of the spaghetti western *Django Kill*. What interested Cox about both films was the depiction of violence and this style can clearly be seen in both *Walker* and *Straight to Hell*.

Before enrolling at Oxford University, Cox took a year out and got a job at a film company called Les Films Marbeuf in Paris. But it wasn't as glamorous as he imagined as Cox was the office boy, sending out invoices and filing receipts. Dispirited, he returned to Merseyside and got a job as a tape editor at the local BBC radio station.

But this was the science-driven Sixties when children were expected to take part in the technological leap forward. The emphasis in schools was on science and engineering. Cox didn't want to spend his time stuck in laboratories and his parents accepted this. Instead, he was encouraged to pursue a 'sensible career' as opposed to working in the arts, and eventually left for Worcester College, Oxford, where he studied Law from 1973 until 1976.

At Oxford, Cox never got lost in academia. Presented with a passionless course of facts, figures and theories, taught by detached professors, he was already looking for a way out. Cox played the game to some extent and recalls an early meeting with the college chaplain to discuss any problems that were troubling him. He told the Reverend Louth he was bored and thinking of changing from Law to Philosophy and Theology, but stressed he didn't want this repeated in case he didn't go ahead with the move. The next morning, as Cox arrived for tutorial, his tutor Francis Reynolds greeted him with, "So Cox, thinking of changing to Philosophy and Theology are you?" Betrayed, he stayed in the Law department but didn't do much work. Instead, he became heavily involved in the theatre, acting in plays such as Joe Orton's *Funeral Games*, *Oh, What a Lovely War* and a production of Peter Barnes' *The Bewitched*. Based on his love of the theatre and films, Cox felt a career in the arts was inevitable.

Making sure he did just enough work to pacify his tutors, Cox devoted the rest of his time to theatrical projects. He directed Philip Franks in Bertolt Brecht's *The*

« Willi Gaminara as Giuseppe 'The Florist' Givola in *The Resistible Rise of Arturo Ui*.

▲ Richard Burton, Peter Bernhard, Philip Franks, Alex Cox, Richard Longworth, Nick Hunt while rehearsing for *The Resistible Rise of Arturo Ui.*

Resistible Rise of Arturo Ui. Franks was a year below Cox, studying English:

> "Alex cast himself in the Brecht play as the actor figure who teaches Ui/Hitler how to exaggerate his movements. He did a very elegant cinematic production, largely based on stills from *Citizen Kane*. It was very impressive. If there had been a drama course available at Oxford, Alex and I would have both been on it. He was always very keen on Jacobean tragedy and once showed me some designs he'd done for a production of *The Duchess of Malfi* that was set in a post-holocaust world with people slithering around in the ruins."

At Oxford, there were no film or drama courses available. If there had been, Cox and many others would have swapped courses at the drop of a hat. Regular movie-going students had to form their own alternative clique, with little or no help from the college administrators.

Franks was part of this Oxford theatre world and got to know Cox well:

> "Alex was an extraordinary figure, very punky with a big brush hairstyle and big staring eyes. He was always obsessed with all things American and so his move to the States was no surprise. He was very energetic, good-natured and rather goofy so the resultant cutting edge and violent films he started off with came as a big surprise because I had always got him pegged as much more benign than that. At Oxford, I always saw him as more of a happy anarchist rather than a snarling savager of society. Years later, I spotted him striding down Wardour Street in Soho, clutching reels and reels of film. One moment he was there and then, suddenly, he'd disappeared into one of the many production offices. Around that time I had seen him on the BBC, introducing *Moviedrome*, and I realised he hadn't changed a bit."

Also while at Oxford, after helping to create a theatre in an old fire station, Cox directed Sam Shepherd's *Geography of a Horse Dreamer*. While scraping through his final

▼ Chorus Line from *Cabaret*, Oxford Playhouse, June 1976

exams, he also managed to gain access to the Playhouse Theatre in Oxford and directed the musical *Cabaret*.

Cox then spent a year at Bristol University as a postgraduate in the Radio, Film and Television Studies department. It wasn't a very enjoyable experience but this was mainly due to the climate:

> "It rained every day and was such a contrast to the idyllic and entertaining world of prizes and people in boaters and top-hats at Oxford. Bristol was very dour and I wasn't at all happy there."

The turning point came in the summer of 1977, when he was turned down for entry to an LWT graduate trainee scheme to become a television producer ("a lucky escape"). Instead, he received a Fullbright Fellowship to study film at UCLA, spending one year in Critical Studies and two in Production. The move to LA was clearly a rebellion against the expectations of others for him to get a "proper job". For Cox, life wasn't purely a financial endeavour and he always intended to develop his artistic side:

> "My family thought I was completely insane at the time because it seemed very unlikely you could get a career in the arts and make any money at it. So although my parents were very pleased that I got the law degree, they were very unhappy that I was going to go off and be a drama queen!"

Although Cox wasn't impressed by Los Angeles, believing it to be "ten times worse than Bristol", he realised that if he was going to make a name for himself in film, whether it be in writing or directing, it was the best place to be. In the end, he stayed in LA for eight years, from 1977 to 1985.

While Cox was at UCLA, he worked as an assistant director on Rose-Marie Turko's *Scarred*, which was begun by Turko and finished with the help of the American Film Institute and National Endowment for the Arts grants. The film was shot by Michael Miner who also shot Cox's student film and later wrote the screenplay for *Robocop*. *Scarred* starred Jennifer Mayo as Ruby Starr, a young girl forced to hit the streets and resort to prostitution to cover her rent and support her child. The character is like a female version of Jon Voight's Buck in *Midnight Cowboy*. The film's merit is in the fact that it wasn't shot in the typical exploitative way and instead showed a positive and aggressive vision of women. Cox can also be seen in *Scarred* as a porno movie actor who is set on by a bunch of women who tie him to the bed and humiliate him, rather than having sex with him. It's a scene in line with the film's feminist riposte to the porno business. Then came Cox's first film as a director.

▲ Setting someone up: Bob Rosen (left) as Smack Hasty and Bill Wood as Ozzie Mamber.

Originally called *Edge City*, one of Cox's friends came up with another title, *Sleep is for Sissies*. He could never decide between the two, so both were used on the final cut – *Edge City* at the beginning, *Sleep is for Sissies* at the end. The budget was $8000, all Cox's own money, which came from various sources during his years at UCLA. He had a part-time teaching assistant job at the university, as well as some paid work in the film archive and $2000 came from a Jack Nicholson Screenwriting Award he received around halfway through his course. All this, together with any loose change, went into financing his 40-minute student film. Most of the film was shot by Michael Miner, who had already been up in a helicopter to shoot a commercial. As a result, Cox bought three aerial shots of LA from Miner for the beginning of the film. Tom Richmond also worked on the film and later shot Cox's spaghetti western, *Straight to Hell*.

Made over two years in LA, *Sleep is for Sissies* is the story of a young artist (Roy Rawlings played by Cox) in society – *Edge City* – otherwise known as Los Angeles. This young limey is going mad in LA, the vile police-obsessed place on the edge of Nothing. The film includes shots of cops beating Latinos on the streets and a demonstration in favour of the Sandanista Revolution.

There is also a variety of other weird characters, including a hippie girl who lives with her dad's old chauffeur in a geodesic dome in Big Sur, a professional assassin who is also a repossessor, a bank robber and some villainous immigration agents. But the film is also very obscure and incomprehensible with a great conclusion – Sid Vicious singing *My Way*.

▲ Bill Wood as Ozzie Mamber in *Edge City* aka *Sleep is for Sissies*.

"In the late Sixties and early Seventies, maybe as far as 1973, films were very interesting. Then films became more conservative. People who had begun their career playing outlaws, Clint Eastwood as the bounty hunter in spaghetti westerns and John Wayne as the Ringo Kid in *Stagecoach*, were ending their careers playing cops. While I thought *Dirty Harry* was a good film, it disturbed me that there seemed to be this systematic inclination of the film industry to push us away from the rebel hero towards the establishment or authoritarian hero. That didn't seem to be a particularly good way to go. It wasn't positive, just a reaction to the Sixties.

"At this point, I was at UCLA and very interested in the punk movement. I'd go and see the British bands when they came over – The Clash, The Jam, 999, The Specials and Selecter – as well as the local Los Angeles groups like Fear, The Circle Jerks and Suicidal Tendencies. With this enthusiasm, I really wanted to make anti-establishment films."

▲ A location for *Edge City* in San Pedro harbour, Los Angeles

But *Sleep is for Sissies* wasn't just a reaction to what was happening in the film industry in the 1970s. Cox felt he should use his time at UCLA to experiment before going out into the 'real world':

> "I actually edited my student film too much. At one point there was a 50-minute version which was sort of intelligible but I was embarrassed by it after a while because the story seemed so mundane. Then I deliberately cut 10 minutes to make it more obscure. It was because I had too much editing time. But the obscure way is always better."

The fractured narrative of *Sleep is for Sissies* is similar to Donald Cammell and Nic Roeg's *Performance* and there is great use of sound layering with dozens of tracks running at the same time. The confusing layers of pre-synthesiser electronic sounds and disturbing voices help create a tense mood and an aura of impending doom, symbolising the chaos of the mind. There are also some great throw-away lines like, "You know I never give advances in advance. What do you know about America anyway?" Interestingly, Harry Dean Stanton was originally going to appear in the film, but then he was offered *Alien*.

» "I never give advances in advance." Bob Rosen as Smack Hasty.

Having finished at UCLA, Cox returned to Britain with his student film, in the hope of getting a screening somewhere. He called the National Film Theatre and tried to persuade them to show the film. But they wanted to know who would be attending. Lindsay Anderson? Nic Roeg? Luckily, both were in the London telephone book at the time, so Cox called them out of the blue, never having met them or spoken to them before. Anderson couldn't make it but Roeg agreed. The screening took place at the NFT in 1981, but because Cox had made only this student film, the only real support system he had was back in the States. He returned to Los Angeles.

After months of rejection letters, money was getting tight. Cox had bills to pay with no regular income. Then, in the spring of 1982, he received an unexpected windfall. After breaking his foot in a motorcycle accident, Cox accepted a $10 000 payment from the insurance company of the woman who had knocked him down. This money kept him going in LA while he looked for work.

Based on the screenplays he had written while at UCLA, Cox managed to find himself an agent, Stephanie Mann. By the end of 1982, she was sending out his scripts and arranging meetings with studio executives for possible screenwriting commissions. However, in order to get his first script-writing job in the highly competitive Hollywood film business, Cox knew he had to make a striking impression and set about organising an incredible stunt. After being called for an interview at MGM/United Artists, the plan was put into action.

Still using crutches because of his motorcycle accident, Cox arranged for his actor

▲ On the streets of LA. Alex Cox as Roy Rawlings in *Edge City*.

friend Ed Pansullo to drive him to the studio. Pansullo was a tough-looking ex-military man who wore a hat with the LAPD logo emblazoned across the front. He lead Cox into the MGM building as if he was a prisoner under arrest. Then, Pansullo started questioning the bemused executives: "I've brought this man for a meeting. Where's the meeting going to take place? Can I see the room? Is the door to the adjacent room locked? Okay!" Finally, he said, "I'm going to be in the corridor. You've got 10 minutes."

During the meeting, with Pansullo waiting outside the door, Cox never referred to him and casually proceeded to pitch the story of Percy Topliss, a World War One deserter who led a revolt against the British army on the eve of Passchendaele. Because of the baffling display put on by the out-of-work pair, the bewildered studio executives were intrigued enough to hire Cox to write the screenplay, *Out of Order Percy*, which he later submitted. After the usual lengthy period of waiting to get paid for the job (a modest $8000), word came back from MGM that they weren't interested in pursuing the project because it was "too English, too expensive and too anti-war". Reagan was now President of the USA and war had once again become an admirable occupation for young Americans. This let-down, and the reasons for rejecting his script, taught Cox a lot about the industry that he was getting into.

After various other meetings with people who didn't give him any work, he was then introduced to the British director Adrian Lyne, who had directed the Jodie Foster film *Foxes*. Lyne told Cox he wanted to make a film about the possibility of nuclear war and that he wanted him to write the screenplay.

▲ "The bureau likes to keep an eye on its foreign visitors." RL Benjamin as the Immigration Official in *Edge City*.

"This was perfect for me because I was obsessed with the subject. I subscribed to the Bulletin of the Atomic Scientists, had Peter Watkins' *The War Game* on video and was pretty much convinced there was going to be a nuclear war, thanks to Thatcher and Reagan, and that I was never going to see my beloved Liverpool again!"

Cox came up with a story, set in Seattle, about a group of people caught up in nuclear war. It was called *The Happy Hour* and Lyne reportedly liked it, had a few minor changes made and then…nothing. Lyne went off to direct *Flashdance*. As a result, Cox is often referred to as the author of that winsome tale. But he is not.

Shortly after the *Happy Hour* incident, Cox met up with two old friends from UCLA – Peter McCarthy and Jonathan Wacks. They had been in the same production programme; Wacks had directed a documentary, McCarthy a dramatic film. They had formed a company in Venice, California, called Wacks–McCarthy which specialised in

▲ Ramon Menendez as the Bank Robber in *Edge City*

❝ The young Alex Cox goes mad in LA.

▲ Bill Wood with a gun in the UCLA parking lot for *Edge City* aka *Sleep is for Sissies*

making commercials ('Gene Kelly assures the public the MGM Grand is safe again!') as well as public service announcements. Cox suggested they should also be feature film producers and hire him as a director. They agreed, on the condition he came up with a script. The first one he submitted was based on a William Burroughs' short story *Exterminator* and was called *The Hot Club*. After budgeting, however, it turned out to be too expensive and so Cox went off to write a second screenplay instead. This one was called *Repo Man*...

Chapter Three

Let's go do some crimes

having gone into partnership with Wacks and McCarthy, Cox was well on the way to making his first feature. Satisfied with the final draft script for *Repo Man*, the film was shopped around for about nine months. Initially, Cox thought he could make it for about $100 000. After all, he'd seen Charles Burnett's *My Brother's Wedding* and *Killer of Sheep*, which were both made for only $10 000. Nevertheless, it proved a struggle to find any funding at all.

It wasn't until he was put in touch with the ex-Monkee and liquid paper king Michael Nesmith that things got off the ground. He was impressed by the originality of the screenplay and presented the film to Universal Pictures who offered a $1.5 million negative pick-up deal. This meant the film had to be delivered on a certain date and if it was a reasonable facsimile of the original script, the film-makers would get their money for it.

By the time the Universal deal was struck, the two leads, Harry Dean Stanton and Emilio Estevez, had already been cast. However, Cox still needed a cameraman. Having seen *The American Friend* and *Kings of the Road*, he wanted Robby Muller. He was sent the script and, according to Cox, he got in touch immediately: "It was generally the script that got people interested, because it was something different." Muller is the Dutch cameraman who also shot most of Wim Wenders' movies, William Friedkin's *To Live and Die in LA*, as well as Jim Jarmusch's *Down by Law* and *Mystery Train*.

Repo Man was shot in six weeks in Los Angeles in late July and August 1983. Over-budget and over-schedule, Cox and the producers had to ask the crew to work for free

▲ The Repo gang listen to the wacky theories of Miller (Tracey Walter).

for the final three days of the shoot. Every crew member elected to stay on. During post-production, however, it was decided an additional day and two extra nights shooting were needed. Peter McCarthy recalls some very arduous re-shoots with virtually no money:

"With a skeleton crew including Bob Richardson behind the camera and Bobby Ellis supervising the stunts, we fixed the opening in the desert (with Al doubling as J Frank in the Malibu), bolstered the coverage of some of the Repo heists, added crashes to Bud chasing the Rodriguez Brothers, got drive-byes of J Frank's Malibu approaching LA and we re-shot much of the final scene of the film which had been replete with holes. When we recreated the Repo yard and pulled off the glowing Malibu effect, using Jerry-rigged $35 beam splitters that matched the original footage, it seemed the arduous task of pick-ups was done and we'd finally gotten everything we needed in the can to finish

the film. We had also utterly exhausted every cent of contingency money and every ounce of goodwill so further re-shoots seemed out of the question."

▲ "Let's do "some crimes…" Debbi (Jennifer Balgobin) and Duke (Dick Rude).

McCarthy's relief was short-lived. Both Cox and the editor Denis Dolan weren't happy with the way Miguel Sandoval's character Archie was killed off. In the original cut, he dies from an arrow shot by Duke (Dick Rude) at a mansion that the punks had broken into. Cox decided he wanted Archie to open the trunk of the Malibu and disintegrate, during a scene in which J Frank tries to get his car back from the punks. As Cox began describing his ideas for yet another re-shoot, McCarthy couldn't hide his utter lack of enthusiasm:

> "We were utterly broke and in danger of being kicked off the film and it was going to be a major deal getting the cast together, rigging the trunk and budgeting another visual effect. My expression must have really troubled Alex because in the midst of his spiel he rose to his feet at the head of the conference

▲ Harry Dean Stanton on the phone as Bud and Emilio Estevez as Otto.

table and boomed in a voice like Moses coming down from the mountain, "PETER, YOU DO NOT BELIEVE!!!" Incredulous, I looked at him and said, "Al, I believe… but I'm tired." We did the re-shoot and Alex was right, vaporising Archie was a much better way to dispose of him."

Repo Man previewed at the Panorama of the Berlin Film Festival in February 1984. Then, a week later, it exploded into American cinemas, immediately registering Alex Cox as one of Britain's most formidable and maverick talents. The film became an instant cult and a star-maker for Emilio Estevez.

An outrageous satire on American culture, *Repo Man* is out of this world. It's a bizarre first feature with an unerring energy that leaves audiences wondering what just happened. Cox presents a series of seemingly unconnected events, beginning with the strange opening scene set on the road from Los Alamos. A highway cop pulls over a Chevy Malibu driven by J Frank Parnell (Fox Harris), a lobotomised scientist, later revealed as the fictitious inventor of the neutron bomb. On the deserted highway, the state trooper asks what is in the trunk. "You don't wanna look in there," replies the

▲ "You don't wanna look in there!"

unstable Parnell. But he ignores this warning and is instantly fried by a bolt of white light. All that remains are the patrolman's smouldering boots. Parnell drives off.

After this odd but symbolic sequence, when the other characters are introduced, and begin to interact with each other, the significance of the Chevy and its driver then comes into play.

The conventional aspects of the film focus on the 'intense' lifestyle of Repo men – freelance operators who steal cars legally. It's the story of a disaffected young punk called Otto (Estevez) who, after quitting his 9–5 supermarket job, meets Bud (Harry Dean Stanton) who tricks him into repossessing a car. After the initial disgust at what he's just done, Otto takes a full-time job as a car repossessor in this seedy LA underworld. He becomes the protégé of Bud who has his own unique philosophy: "Ordinary people. I hate 'em." After teaching him the ropes, Otto soon learns enough to challenge his mentor for the $20 000 1964 Chevy Malibu together with the sinister contents of its trunk.

The offbeat nature of the film concerns the race for the Chevy – and the prize money. But as well as Otto and Bud, there are other pursuers: government agents, amateur UFO investigators and the infamous Rodriguez Brothers. None of them realises the glowing contents of the trunk could change the course of civilisation – overnight.

▲ Duke, Debbi and the soon to be vaporised Archie.

Zander Schloss, who plays geeky teenager Kevin, says he owes his entire career to Alex Cox. In the early Eighties, when Cox was still working on the script, fellow punk Schloss was living in his car and working at a health food store, stealing groceries for them both to eat. Initially, Cox gave him a job as a PA. Sean Penn's brother Chris was to play Kevin but producer, Michael Nesmith, wasn't impressed with what he saw. Schloss was thrown in at the deep end, with no acting experience: "I went from having to pick up cigarette butts on the parking lot to having my own trailer with a star on it!" Having been part of the Circle Jerks, who played on the *Repo Man* soundtrack, Schloss went on to co-produce the score for *Sid & Nancy* and played Karl in *Straight to Hell*, where he developed a strong working relationship with ex-Clash member Joe Strummer. They both went on to compose the score for Cox's *Walker*.

The character of Otto is brilliantly underplayed by Emilio Estevez and Harry Dean Stanton is perfect in the role of Bud, the veteran Repo man giving out words of wisdom like, "An ordinary person spends life avoiding tense situations. Repo man spends his life getting into tense situations."

"Originally, we wanted to have Dennis Hopper play the part of Bud. When I had finished the final draft,

Peter McCarthy and I drove to New Mexico to look for Dennis at an art gallery there called The Return run by his brother David. He wasn't there but we did manage to get a contact address for him in Los Angeles so we could arrange a meeting. Eventually, we met up with Dennis and his agent at a restaurant and found him a really fascinating guy who was quite interested in playing the part. But in the end it came down to money and we just couldn't afford what he was asking for.

"Fortunately, I also knew this other actor called Harry Dean Stanton. When I was a student at UCLA, I tried to get him to be in my student film. A friend of mine, Tom Musca, worked in a restaurant at the top of Beverly Glen and Mulholland Drive called Santo Pietro Pizza. So he would call me when Harry Dean came in to eat and I'd race up there on my motorcycle and the spiel would start "Ah, Harry Dean, what a surprise. I too always dine here." Tom would give me a piece of free pizza and I would chat up Harry Dean. In the end, he didn't do my student film but we got on well and later he agreed to do *Repo Man*. Similarly, I met Sy Richardson through UCLA when he was acting in Monona Wali's student film *The Grey Area*. On set, I could see that this guy was just outstanding. His power was enormous. And he was also very sensitive compared with Harry Dean who always seemed to be a great actor but somewhat pampered. Sy, on the other hand, had great integrity and was always supportive given my inexperience.

"As for Emilio Estevez, I had seen him in a Francis Ford Coppola film called *The Outsiders* and although he only had a small part, he had a little improvisation where they kept the camera rolling at the end of a scene. He goes to the refrigerator and pulls out a bottle of beer and a big chocolate cake. He then sits down and proceeds to drink the beer and eat the entire cake. I thought, "That's good. I can relate to that. This is a chap I would like to work with one day." I think he had the potential to be a very interesting actor but the choices he's made since *Repo Man* were not congruent with that."

▲ Eddie Velez (left) and Del Zamora as the Rodriguez Brothers, Napoleon and Lagarto

Cox's world of urban chaos and absurd behaviour is similar in style, narrative and dialogue to many of the 1950s and 1960s B movies. It has obvious allusions to Robert Aldrich's classic of late film noir, *Kiss Me Deadly* (1955), a loose adaptation of one of Mickey Spillane's *Mike Hammer* thrillers with Ralph Meeker as a sleazy Hammer, on the trail of 'the great whatsit' (a box filled with a radioactive substance), who'll use violence to stop anyone who gets in his way. It's clear Aldrich is actually criticising Spillane's macho style and the nuclear paranoia of Fifties America. With *Repo Man*, Cox has captured the same sense of anxiety about some sort of mysterious force at work in a civilisation on the edge of the apocalypse.

"On the basis of my experiences with Mark Lewis, a real Repo man, I wrote the original script for *Repo Man* in 1983, but at that time it was a road movie and another rather expensive thing which started off in Los Angeles and went all the way out across New Mexico. It ended up in the city of Truth Or Consequences, New Mexico, for a startling finale involving an atomic bomb which was what was in the trunk of the Chevy at the time. That again looked like it was going to be too expensive so at a certain point I dropped the road movie element and instead concentrated the whole film in Los Angeles and at the same time added the 'what's in the trunk?' gag which is parallel to that of *Kiss Me Deadly* where you have Mike Hammer with the plot of 'what's in the mysterious box?'

"The 1954 film *Them!* also influenced *Repo Man*. It's a film about a colony of giant ants in the desert who have grown up as a result of nuclear testing. It begins in the Joshua Tree monument in the desert outside Palmdale where *Repo Man* begins and ends in the famous storm drains of Los Angeles which are also prominently featured in *Repo Man*. *Them!* is one of a whole sub-genre of science fiction films that were made in the 1950s in the aftermath of the atomic bomb. The theme of these films is pretty constant: science gone wrong. In Britain, around the same time, we were doing stuff like the *Quatermass* TV series and, later, the *Quatermass* films. In the US, films such as *Them!*, *Forbidden Planet* and *The Incredible Shrinking Man* all skirted around the same theme. They all deal with the atom bomb and nuclear testing. In *This Island Earth*, an alien planet has been destroyed by years of nuclear war; in *The Incredible Shrinking Man*, the hero, Scott Carey, passes through a radioactive mist and incredibly…starts to shrink. All of this sounds pretty funny, and it is quite funny. However, it's worth pointing out that, as the Americans embarked on the Korean war, taking us with it, and as the US, the Soviet Union, France and Britain began amassing huge stockpiles of nuclear weapons, and as Eisenhower warned about the build-up of a 'military–industrial complex', the only films that addressed the issue were a handful of baroque science-fiction movies – most of them directed by Jack Arnold. They were very cheaply made, funny, visionary and intelligent. They have good scripts as well. *The Incredible Shrinking Man* was written by Richard Matheson who wrote a lot of first-rate fantasy and science fiction, including the novel on which *The Omega Man* is based.

▲ "A Repo man is always intense…but only a fool would get killed for a car." Otto (Emilio Estevez) learns the trade from Lite (Sy Richardson).

"Don Siegel's 1956 cult film *Invasion of the Body Snatchers* is, like Robert Aldrich's *Kiss Me Deadly*, a film that exists on the borderline between science fiction and film noir. Siegel's theme was the substitution of red-blooded Americans by mindless, alien clones and has been described as a metaphor for the witch hunts of the McCarthy era and, more recently, as an exercise in red-baiting, anti-Communism. At the time, the great manufactured paranoia was Communism, and the film could be viewed as a warning against said political doctrine, or as a criticism of those who would suppress it at all costs. Aldrich's *Kiss Me Deadly*, about a stolen nuclear bomb, is a similar film noir. Robert Aldrich, when he wanted to, could be an old style tough-guy director. His most popular work is probably *The Dirty Dozen*. He's the sort of director that gets called 'efficient' or 'a good craftsman' – that is, stylistically his films don't break new ground, but they have good

▲ "It happens sometimes. People just explode. Natural causes."

stories. He is a good director of actors and knows the power of the empty frame. Aldrich's black-and-white films generally look great and *Kiss Me Deadly* is his one great film. His colour films, such as *The Grissom Gang*, are for some reason always too brightly lit, like television comedies.

"*Repo Man* was really a combination of the plot of an American film noir like *Kiss Me Deadly* or an American science fiction movie of the 1950s along with my impressions of Los Angeles and all this *Repo Man* texture I'd picked up from Mark Lewis. Mark lived with the actor Ed Pansullo around the corner from me. They lived on Venice Boulevard and I lived over on Penmar. I began to drive around with Mark and observed him, his impressions of the world and the code of the Repo man. I did, on one or two occasions, drive his car back while he drove the repossessed car back. So I was his accomplice who thought it was all very wicked and immoral, but then began to enjoy stealing people's cars! Eventually the script went through 14 drafts before the producers and I were happy with it.

"A big turning point was when Abbe Wool introduced us to a producer called Harry Gittes, who, in turn, introduced us to the former Monkee Michael Nesmith. At one point, he was going to fund the film out of his own pocket because he was wealthy at the time. He liked the script because he'd had experiences with car repossessors. I then met the repossessors responsible for taking away his car and found very different versions of the same story! But I think Nesmith was also intrigued by the comic book aspect of the project. In order to sell the script and make it appear more attractive I had put four pages of comic book that I had drawn at the beginning of the screenplay. My original plan was to do the whole thing as a comic book but it was too much work: a page a day at the very most, hard on the eyes, and I was just too lazy. At one point we were going to turn the script into a cartoon and then back to a live action piece, but that never happened.

"When Michael Nesmith decided not to fund the film himself, he took it to Universal Studios. Luckily for us there was a strange corporate attitude prevailing there at the time. The Head of Production was Bob Rehme who had come from the Corman empire and believed in funding a lot of films, in the expectation that some of them would fail and some of them would make money. This was quite an exceptional attitude based on the idea that if you cast a wide net and hire some interesting directors, you might get back some bad films but you might get back some great ones too. So Rehme did this with *Repo Man*, taking it as a 'negative pick-up' which means that the studio will fund a film when it's finished. When they see the finished film and like it, they guarantee to pay a certain amount to acquire the negative. The producers go to the bank to borrow the money to make the film against the eventual promise of cash from the studio.

▲ Magic Tree Air Freshener: "You find one in every car."

"Sadly, while we were in post-production, a regime change happened at Universal. Rehme was ousted from his post, and a new boss called Frank Price came in. As always in these cases, the new guy had to make the person who previously held his chair look bad. So all the films Universal had made were doomed at that point. Some of them, like *Streets of Fire*, which cost $20 million, did get a release in an attempt to recoup. But with cheaper films like *Repo Man* and interestingly *Rumblefish*, which Coppola had made back-to-back with *The Outsiders*, had to be dumped because they pissed off the executives. But even while they were trying to dump it, the cinematographer Robby Muller had managed to get the film shown at the Berlin Film Festival where it got a very good response. It was then shown for a week in Los Angeles and for a week in Chicago. As far as Universal were concerned, that was it and it would go straight to video. Indeed it did.

> "In response, we took out an ad in Variety, reprinting a good review we got there as a challenge to get the picture out in the theatres. The studio still didn't want to know and certain executives condemned the film. The studio also brought in the head of public relations at Pan American World Airlines to denounce the film. PanAm had some sort of deal with Universal to show all their films on flights. The PR man was called Dick Barkle who said how shocked he was and how he hoped the film wouldn't be shown in Russia!
>
> "But at the same time, there was also a soundtrack album out which the producers Peter McCarthy and Jonathan Wacks had put together. It was made up of all the music from the film and was selling briskly. So the record division of MCA–Universal wanted to know more about the film. Someone who worked for this record division, Kelly Neal, really liked *Repo Man* and *Rumblefish* and he promoted the film more than anyone else at Universal. The punks then got to hear of it through the soundtrack and word spread from there. And so began the revival of *Repo Man* in the cinemas."

With *Repo Man*, Cox set out to produce something radically different. This wickedly funny film is so refreshing when compared with the vast amount of utterly trivial and superficial comedies of the 1980s. Alex Cox's screenplay is a dazzling piece of writing which extends the boundaries of comedy. His anarchistic method of directing is distinguished by its dark energy and means the viewer is always left breathless. Nothing is predictable.

The film can be watched on various levels. On the surface, *Repo Man* is a bizarre black comedy with more to offer than the other bland American comedies of that period. But at a deeper level, the film is a satire on American culture: consumerism, TV-evangelism and government conspiracies.

Cox focuses on the struggle for individual survival in a modern world that favours the mass. The world is grey where consumerism has taken over. Kevin, Otto's friend at the supermarket, can't stop singing the theme from the 7-Up commercials. The characters have names like Miller and Bud, the brand names of beers, hinting that we are all commodities. Even products used in the film are actually given generic labels 'Food' and 'Beer'. When Otto returns home one night, his parents are sitting in the living room, hypnotised by a TV evangelist. They tell him they've sent all of his college fund to Reverend Larry so it can be used to send bibles to El Salvador. His mother tells him to put his canned 'Food' on a plate so he'll enjoy it more.

▲ J Frank Parnell (Fox Harris) confronted by Duke (Dick Rude).

Repo Man is also about personal codes and philosophies and how, in modern society, personal ethics are being replaced by the notion of personal gain. In *Repo Man*, the only characters who rise above this hell are the Repo men – Bud, Otto, Miller and Lite. "Not many people got a code to live by anymore," says Bud, voicing his battle with the outside world. Miller (Tracey Walter) is probably the most well-rounded character in the film. At first, he is introduced as an extremely eccentric character, uttering weird personal theories such as, "The more you drive, the less intelligent you are," and we are invited to laugh at him, but as the film progresses, it is made clear that he is the one with the right ideas and by the end we are laughing with him. It is Bud, and these other Repo men, who come to represent a better way than consumer culture. They are the people who come to separate 'ordinary people' from their number one material possession – the car. They take away the prize of upward mobility and subsequently, in the spaced-out finale, Otto and Miller themselves literally become highly upwardly mobile.

The film is therefore about rebellion and, with its killer West Coast punk soundtrack, *Repo Man* was a real hit with punk audiences. However, Cox even pokes fun at this backdrop of punk rock by having Otto's friend, Duke die during a convenience store robbery. His final words: "I know a life of crime led me to this sorry fate. And yet, I blame society. Society made me what I am," are exposed as a cop out when Otto replies, "That's bullshit. You're a white suburban punk, just like me."

The soundtrack isn't simply therefore used to just sell the film but, according to Cox, it is a vital part of the film that helps to convey Otto's culture:

> "Like all those Valley punks, he's a middle-class kid from a 'nice' home who listens to all this hardcore, angry music. He's angry without really knowing why."

Originally, Cox wanted the Clash but their manager got in the way. At the same time, Iggy Pop's manager requested to see the film and, as soon as he saw it, Iggy agreed to record the title track. The soundtrack was kept a secret from Michael Nesmith as he was by no means a fan of punk rock: "At the time, his favourite was Jimmy Buffet, you see, but we stuck to our guns," explains Cox.

Repo Man is not just another Hollywood product. Order is disturbed and therefore audience's assumptions about the conventions of cinema are also disturbed. Cox combines the car chase plot with punk music, gang themes and a sci-fi conclusion. It is a rare example of a film-maker truly refusing to be bound by traditional convention. By acknowledging the idea of naff branding and consumerism within the film, Cox is pushing the fact that this film is different. This is not to say he went out intentionally to make a 'cult' film.

> "At first, I found the idea of *Repo Man* gaining this cult audience quite odd and I really hadn't expected that to happen. Having analysed it, I think in a certain way it's a compendium of weird ephemera. The film does have a lot of modern myths in it such as the idea that people can self-combust, that they can spontaneously explode while sitting in an armchair and the idea of all this stolen nuclear material and weird poison drifting around. Not to mention the pop culture aspects of punk rock. I think the monologues of Sy and Tracey Walter added to it. For example, Tracey's character Miller talks about flying saucers really being time-machines and that all the disappeared people in Latin America have actually vanished into the past. It's a bit like in *Men In Black* where they say all the real news of this planet can actually be found in *The Weekly World News*, that very funny American tabloid about aliens voting for Clinton and so on. *Repo Man* serves exactly the same purpose in that I was saying,

▲ A punk in a suit.
Emilio Estevez as Otto Parts.

"This is where the actual true information is. These things really do exist…"

"Or do they?

"My other belief is that all of this flying saucer stuff is just a cover for black aviation projects or moving nuclear material around at the dead of night. *Repo Man* was actually going to deal more with this but, at the eleventh hour, I changed the script to give it a more positive spin. This happened because of the importance Tracey Walter's character had taken on during the shooting. The Repo people really did become a group. It wasn't just Harry Dean. They all had weight in the film and in the end Tracey became the most important of all. This group of legal thieves are there in Los Angeles, a place obsessed with the car, where people are judged by the car they drive, actually taking cars away from people.

"However, I hope it becomes clear that all of the

characters' own personal philosophies are bogus. Everybody is telling you their philosophy. Tracey's, Sy's and Harry Dean's philosophies are all very strongly felt but they are bogus. Even the punk culture in the film is really bogus. Otto instantly goes from being a rebellious, anarchic, anti-establishment punk to being an enforcer for the General Motors Acceptance Corporation. He doesn't even have to change his appearance. He looks exactly the same in both cultures, whether he's wearing a Suicidal Tendencies T-shirt or a suit. The other punks, Duke, Debbi and Archie are just a loathsome bunch of liquor store hold-up artists sniffing butyl nitrate. Then there's The Circle Jerks, a former hard-core punk group, who have become an awful lounge band like you'd find in some terrible club in Las Vegas. The point of all that is that youth culture is bogus too. It's merely a means for people to make money.

"Strangely, the film's success was down, in part, to the weird genre-busting. Usually that kind of anarchic film-making upsets audiences. But in this instance, it somehow hung together tightly enough so that people weren't offended by it, despite what the Universal studio executives might think. The studio decided they would make their own re-edited broadcast TV video version of *Repo Man* because of the swearing and the scene of speed-snorting. When they had done all of their cuts, the film was down to about 60 minutes. It was all very odd because it was as if these guys were trying to 'explain' the film. They were puzzled. In their version they included extra shots of the licence plate of the Chevy Malibu. It was a New Mexico licence plate with a Hopi symbol in the centre of it. But what they had done was to shoot static shots of the car and intercut them with sequences where the car is moving, which looked really bad. Then, on the licence plate, the Hopi symbol turned into the horned skull of Satan! It's true! The Hollywood studios really are run by Satanists. They were putting their devil-worshipping propaganda in my film!

"I was inclined to leave it alone because this TV version was the worst dog's breakfast piece of rubbish.

▲ Agent Rogers (Susan Barnes) shows off her metal hand.

But Dick Rude persuaded me I should make an effort to fix it. We opened up the rushes that we had cut out and put in a couple of scenes which weren't in the original version: the one with Jac MacNally shaving (where Harry Dean says his name is IG Farben) and the one where Harry Dean smashes the phone booth with his baseball bat. The British broadcast version is a melange of the two and does have much of the swearing, but not all of it. It was interesting what we did with the swearing. We had to come up with alternative words so instead of saying "Mother Fucker" they'd say "Melon Farmer" which I thought was really funny anyway. In fact, it made it funnier. I didn't mind because after *Sid & Nancy* I was just so sick of swearing. The actors also got paid an extra day to come in and re-record the new words – so everyone was happy.

"I have become more involved in the creation of video versions because, in the end, more people will see my films on video. Even a film like *Titanic* will be seen by more people via television and video than through people visiting their local cinema.

"What also happens in video versions is if the distribution doesn't care about the product, they will fail to letterbox or scan the print: sometimes microphones and dolly tracks are left in the bottom or the top of the screen which obviously shouldn't be there. Ironically, when they are left in the videos of my films, it's viewed as another example of my wacky and anarchistic style of direction. Actually, when you see the dolly tracks in the *Repo Man* video (in the scene before the liquor store robbery) it's very funny, even though Robby never wanted them to be seen. Maybe I should have done it deliberately!"

Repo Man undoubtedly found an audience because the punk movement was still alive at the time of its release. The film is infused with the spirit of punk. Bands like Black Flag, Suicidal Tendencies, Fear and The Circle Jerks dominate the soundtrack and the incidental music is provided by two members of The Plugz, Tito Larriva and Steven Hufsteter. They are responsible for the extraordinary Morricone-esque final track.

Understandably, there were a lot of people who were either punks, or were the brothers or sisters of punks, who got behind the film because it had that anti-establishment flavour. Cox's familiarity with the punk scene is certainly impressive and continued with his next film...

Chapter Four

Never trust a junkie

If I asked you to kill me, would you?

"The definitive pic on the punk phenomenon...
both actors are beyond praise...
a dynamic piece of work."
Variety

After *Repo Man*, word reached Alex Cox that a Hollywood film was going to be made about the lives of Sex Pistols' bassist Sid Vicious and his groupie girlfriend Nancy Spungen. The cast would include Madonna and Rupert Everett.

Cox wasn't impressed. With an intense interest in the punk movement and his own opinions of how Sid and Nancy became traitors to a revolutionary movement, he desperately wanted to tell their story before a Hollywood studio did. Cox was always interested in the story of the two lovers rather than the story of the Sex Pistols. The story of the band had already been made as *The Great Rock 'n' Roll Swindle*, directed by Julien Temple.

There is no doubt the story of Sid Vicious and Nancy Spungen is one of the most sensational in rock history. On October 12th 1978, as his girlfriend's body lay in a pool of blood on the bathroom floor of Room 101 in New York's Chelsea Hotel, Sid Vicious was in the bedroom, drenched in blood. Four months later, he died of a heroin

overdose while awaiting trial for Nancy Spungen's murder. He had been released on bail in New York City just 24 hours earlier.

« The real Sid Vicious, 1978

Cox had already written a script called *Too Kool to Die* in 1980. It wasn't about Sid and Nancy but did involve a fictional band and a murder. Up until the news of a possible Hollywood biopic of Sid and Nancy, he hadn't taken this script any further. Now the time was right. He began developing his early script and, together with Abbe Wool, started researching the doomed lovers' story. As one of Cox's fellow UCLA punk rocker pals, Wool had read the *Too Kool to Die* script before any plans for a movie about Sid and Nancy:

> "Of course, no one else in the legitimate film-making world would even look at it, but I thought it was great. Although it was a fictitious rendering of the romance between Sid and Nancy, it was still about the demise of English punk rock. The script we later co-wrote for *Sid & Nancy* was a mixture of reality and a cartoon-like version of events."

Wool and Cox were romantically involved during their time at film school and while Cox made *Repo Man*. The pair actually married in between *Repo Man* and *Sid & Nancy*, although by this time they were simply work colleagues rather than lovers, with the marriage more about Cox being able to secure his visa to work in the US. Wool has since retired from writing and directing and has become a movie electrician:

> "There's more real happiness in film-making below the line than above it. I have less hassle now but with the same amount of fun and, for the most part, meet a better quality of people. I'm still amazed though at how many people comment on *Sid & Nancy*. It made such an impression which is a really nice feeling for me. Even better is that people are still talking about the real Sid and Nancy. After all, they lived the life. Alex and I just wrote it down."

Most of the principal research was done in London. Cox and Wool spoke to a lot of people who had known Sid and Nancy, including Debbie Wilson, Malcolm McLaren and Lech Kowalski who had directed the documentary *DOA* about the punk movement with an over-the-edge interview with Sid and Nancy. Cox and Wool also spoke to Sid's mother. The screenplay was based on these interviews as well as various newspaper articles written about the pair. They stayed away from Nancy's mother's book which Cox saw as lacking in a certain clarity and self-knowledge:

> "It seemed like she was incapable of taking any responsibility for the person that Nancy had been. She was treated rather like she was Linda Blair in *The Exorcist* and I thought perhaps you could find a more substantial reason as to why she was so disturbed."

Around this time, while *Repo Man* was playing in theatres in the UK, Cox bumped into a young video producer called Eric Fellner. He was responsible for a variety of pop promos in the Eighties, most famously the Duran Duran videos. Fellner knew how to obtain money for video productions and had some technical expertise. However, at the age of 25, he was already bored with music videos and wanted to produce a feature film. He sold his company, went to Africa for six months, returned to London and had business cards printed which said 'Eric Fellner – Film Producer' as opposed to 'Eric Fellner – Video Producer'. At a bar in central London, Cox and Fellner exchanged numbers.

When the *Sid & Nancy* script hit Fellner's desk, with its combination of drama and music, he realised it was the perfect project to get involved in:

> "I thought the script was adventurous and exciting, although at the time, I didn't really realise just how daring it was because I didn't have enough scripts to compare it with. I made a commitment to Alex to get the film financed because he was just so passionate about what he wanted to do, and that enthusiasm rubbed off on me. After meeting him, I knew that he was someone I wanted to do business with. He was someone I would've spent 24 hours a day, seven days a week with, just to get the film made. I also met his partner at the time, Abbe Wool, and thought the same about her. We all believed in it."

During one early meeting, Cox informed Fellner he wouldn't option the film to him because he didn't want to get tied up with one person:

> "That's the way Alex works, and I agreed to this condition because I didn't know what the fuck he was talking about and had no concept of what that meant. Today, I would never start working on a project unless I controlled the rights. Only later did I realise that having spent a year working on *Sid & Nancy*, Alex could easily have gone off and done it with someone else. It's only

recently that I found out how many other producers were trying to put the film together."

Cox recalls differently.

"Of course we went out to different financiers but Eric was the only producer we ever had in mind. It would have been completely impossible to make it without him."

Margaret Matheson, Head of Production at Zenith, worked alongside Eric Fellner and put the finance together. A fairly modest budget of $4 million was allocated for the 11-week shoot, which came from both Zenith Productions, in London, and Embassy Home Entertainment, in Los Angeles. It was Matheson's love of the script that prompted her to go straight ahead with backing the film:

"Unbelievably, the choice of films we did at Zenith was down to what I liked personally rather than conducting huge marketing surveys, and fortunately, *Sid & Nancy* touched a nerve with a substantial and faithful audience."

Matheson gave Cox carte blanche in casting, which meant he could cast unknown actors, even for the two lead roles. Everyone auditioned: Gary Oldman, Chloe Webb, David Hayman, Xander Berkeley – just as the actors had on *Repo Man*. The only person who said no to a part was Tim Roth, who was asked to play Johnny Rotten, but felt it was too close to recent history. For the part of Nancy, an open-call audition was advertised in *Maximumrocknroll* and *Flipside*. More than 500 bleached blondes turned up to play the scene where Nancy sees her image in a mirror and shrieks, "Sid! Help me! I look like fuckin' Stevie Nicks in hippie clothes!"

A then-unknown Courtney Love could relate to the part, and with no acting experience, she called co-writer Abbe Wool at home, insisting she be given a chance to audition. She turned up with an entourage of punks and impressed the producer, Peter McCarthy with her reading:

"Courtney came in wearing only a loose cotton dress with no shoes on and incredibly dirty feet. She was like a puppet without strings, all over the place and very funny. She did such a kick-ass reading."

Love was one of the few actresses to be called back. Cox agreed that she had obvious talent but felt that without the same level of experience as Gary Oldman, she wouldn't be able to hold her own in that duo. Instead, she was given a small role,

"It's part of Alex's way to go against convention like when he puts Joe Strummer's salsa music over the action sequences in *Walker*. He does it in imagery as well, like putting kittens in a punk rock club!".
Director, actor and kitten.

playing one of Nancy's junkie friends, Gretchen. Cox had written the part for Love but then had to track her down after discovering she had landed a job at Brandy How's strip club in Guam. She escaped and returned to New York City.

According to McCarthy, during breaks in filming in New York, Love would spend her wages on a fortune-teller, even though she was broke: "I think she thought that this was such a pivotal point in her life and that everything was going to change from here on in." Cox also allowed Love to help cast extras and gave her friend Joe Mama a job in wardrobe. The following year, she went on to co-star in Cox's next film *Straight to Hell*.

At the London auditions for *Sid & Nancy*, Cox was impressed by a young Kathy Burke. He was the first film director to make proper use of her, offering her the part of a Pistols hanger-on, Brenda, and the opportunity to work with Gary Oldman. A decade later, she teamed up with Oldman again to co-star in his directorial debut *Nil by Mouth*, for which she won the Best Actress award at Cannes in 1997.

Another actor who met with Cox to discuss playing the part of Sid was Daniel Day Lewis, another then-unknown London stage actor. Cox decided on Oldman because he was from the same part of London as Sid and understood the ambitious aspect of his character; the need to get out of South London at all costs:

> "He hadn't done any movies at that time and he was desperate to be in one. Gary did a great job in a very demanding role; but his father died while we were filming, so it was a very difficult time for him."

DIARY OF ALEX COX THE MAKING OF *SID & NANCY*

Too Kool to Die was the tale of a blind, implacable detective (modelled after Gilbert Shelton's 'Tricky Prickears'), hired by a rich American family to rescue their daughter, Adele, from the clutches of an English bass player, Ringo Shiv. The piece was quite surreal and was mostly about the corruption of the punk movement and the peculiar political circumstances in England just before the Thatcher nightmare. It involved the flooding of London, the Jeremy Thorpe scandal, the Shah of Iran's heroin dealing and other things that guaranteed it never would be made. Structurally, it has some things in common with the script Abbe Wool and I wrote five years later *Love Kills*.

What follows is a record of the progress of that film. I have included some of the diary references to rock and roll shows attended, films seen at the cinema and motorbikes.

1985

7 Jan — Circle Jerks, CBGBs.

10 Jan — Repo Man opens in London. I am at Chelsea Hotel in New York interviewing people who knew Sid and Nancy: Lech Kowalski, James Spacely, Heidi, Rita...

14 Jan — Finish 'Sid' outline.

15 Jan Start writing script.
19 Jan Screamin' Jay Hawkins, Birdland West.
20 Jan See *Blood Simple*.
23 Jan Finish first draft.
24 Jan Meet Ann Beverly, Sid's mum, Hole in Wall pub, Waterloo.
25 Jan With Debbie Wilson and Alan Jones re: Sid. Meet William Burroughs, with James Grauerholtz, his ward.
27 Jan See *Secret Honor*.
28 Jan *Repo Man* plays at the Luxor, Rotterdam. Meet Rudy Wurlitzer, with Harry Dean Stanton, his ward.
2 Feb Anniversary of Sid Vicious' death. Last night of Rotterdam Film Festival. Party.
4 Feb Abbe Wool arrives in London for second draft. Stationed at 84c Lupus Street, Pimlico.
13 Feb Finish second draft *Love Kills*. Meet Eric Fellner, Nicky Hart, Sun in Splendour?
1 Mar Hired by Orion Pictures to write *Mars Attacks!*
23 Mar See Pogues, Liverpool Polytechnic. Adelphi Hotel.
29 Mar Untouchables, Dingwalls.
31 Mar Meet Dave Bridges, Location scout.
1 April Meet Margaret Matheson, Zenith Productions.
2 April Shoot *A Pair of Brown Eyes* video for the Pogues in Golders Green Tube, Hampstead Heath/Pastoral Idyll, Electric Ballroom.
3 April Shoot for *Brown Eyes* continues. Kings Cross Snooker Club, Anchor Pub, Bankside, Southwark Market.
4 April Shoot studio pub effects.
8 April Pogues, Men They Couldn't Hang, Billy Brag, Mean Fiddler, Harlesden.
12 April Deliver *Brown Eyes* video to Robbo, Island in Shakespeare Head, Carnaby Street. *Lower Depths*, Young Vic Theatre with Walter Donaghue. 1000 Mexicans, Electric.
13 April Flaco Jimenez, Half Moon, Putney.
14 April See *In the Name of the People*, *Brazil*, Stoke Newington.
10 May Eric and I sign up with Zenith. Eric will budget, produce picture. Zenith (Margaret M, Charles Denton, Scott Meek) will provide 50% finance, seek the rest.
14 May Rent flat, nay, artist's loft at Neckinger Mills, 164 Abbey Street, Bermondsey.
16 May With Edward Tudor Pole, Tower Bridge.
18 May Request interview with Johnny Thunders; he requests fee; decide against.
19 May With Linda Ashby, Man in the Moon.
28 May Buy *Django Kill* beta tape, Tottenham Court Road.
31 May Borrow J Thomas' Moto Guzzi – '84 V50/3.
1 June *Mars Attacks!* first draft due.
4 June London casting begins – Lucy Boulding.

5 June Potato Exhibition and Sampling at the Waldorf Hotel, Aldwich (Adelphi Suite).

19 June Meet Glen Matlock, at Zenith. Last night of *Repo Man* in London.

23 June Buy '83 BMW R100RT motorbike, Cowley.

28 June In Los Angeles, at Kensington Hotel. Rent '65 Plymouth Valiant. See Vicky Thomas, re: Los Angeles casting. See Peter McCarthy and Debbie Diaz re: US production.

1 July Begin week of casting in LA.

5 July See *Emerald Forest*, Plitt, Century City.

6 July See *Rambo*, *Pale Rider.*

8 July Readings; to London.

9 July *Love Kills* office open, 52 Tottenham Street.

10 July London auditions begin.

11 July See *1984*, Charing Cross Road.

15 July PRE-PRODUCTION BEGINS.

17 July See *War Plays*, Barbican – four and a half hours!

19 July Read Dan Day Lewis; to Anna Sher School.

20 July See *Duchess of Malfi*, Lyttleton, National Theatre.

22 July Read Gary Oldman, Pete Lee Wilson, Lee Drysdale. See *Grafters*, Hampstead.

26 July Read McClarens, Pistols.

29 July See *My Beautiful Launderette*.

30 July Pogues reception, HMS Belfast.

31 July To New York.

1 Aug Meet Gary Kerferst. Interview Dee Dee Ramone, Queens.

2, 3 Aug Actor meetings.

4 Aug Meet Joe Stevens, Sid photographer, Hudson. To London.

7 Aug Pogues, Men, Boothills, Costello Nicaragua Benefit, Fridge, Brixton.

9 Aug Embassy Home Entertainment offer Zenith $1 750 000 for US rights to *Love Kills*. Eric and Margaret reckon we need $1 822 000. Lunch with Gary Oldman, Soho.

10 Aug See *Element of Crime*, Scala.

12 Aug See *Are You Lonesome Tonight?* by Alan Bleasdale.

14 Aug Read Lindas; to Los Angeles.

16 Aug Meet Lee Katz, Completion Bond Co. Nancy meetings.

17 Aug Nancy meetings.

18 Aug Nancy meetings; read Patty Tippo; Courtney Love.

21 Aug Nancys: tape Courtney, Chloe, Lisa.

23 Aug To New York; location scout.

26 Aug To London.

27 Aug Meet Roger Deakins.

28 Aug New offices; 21 Harrington Rd, SW7.

29 Aug Location scout.

30 Aug Read Lindas, Phoebes, Rottens, Joneses, Cooks.

31 Aug To Los Angeles.

1 Sept Read Nancys.

2 Sept To New York; readings.

3 Sept Readings; to London.

6 Sept Location scout with Paul Rafael, Roger Deakins.

9 Sept Meet David Martin, Editor; location scout.

10 Sept Meet Peter Glossop, Sound Recordist.

11 Sept To Los Angeles for more location scouts.

14 Sept To New York for lawyers meeting (1030–1845 hrs); Read Jim Carrol; David Johansen. See Buster Poindexter, 15th & Irving.

15 Sept Meet John Lydon, 1800 hrs, Mayflower Hotel. To London.

16 Sept Meet Drew Schofield, Glen Matlock, 6 Denmark Street.

17 Sept Rehearse with Chloe and Gary.

18 Sept Cast read through.

29 Sept Billy Bragg Nicaragua Benefit, Academy, Brixton.

22 Sept Hair meeting; Dinner with Chloe, Ann, Paul Mavrides, Gilbert Shelton. Pogues, Hammersmith Palais.

24 Sept Principals' costume meeting.

25 Sept Make-up meeting; screen original Bill Grundy interview for actors.

26 Sept Videotape our 'Grundy' interview.

30 Sept PRODUCTION STARTS – WEEK ONE – Linda's pad.

1 Oct Linda's pad, cont.

2 Oct Buckingham Palace Road, Taxi Ride, Trafalgar Square, Harrods.

3 Oct Linda's.

4 Oct Linda's.

5 Oct (day off) Location scout; to Gaudy, Worcester College.

7 Oct WEEK TWO – Belgravia, Int & Ext.

8 Oct Belgravia, Int.

9 Oct Cambridge Circus.

10 Oct Clissold Road, Albion Road, Vivisection Lab.

11 Oct Seditionaries (Scenes 44 & 73).

12 Oct Anniversary of Nancy's death. Location scout; recording studio with Gary.

14 Oct WEEK THREE – Paradise Club.

15 Oct Recording studio.

16 Oct Boat Trip, Thames.

17 Oct Phone Box and rest of Boat Trip (Scene 39).

18 Oct Int. Van, Uxbridge/Winterland.

20 Oct Re-record vocals, sound suite.

21 Oct WEEK FOUR – Crest Hotel, Glitterbest, Old Mahon Ext.

22 Oct Old Mahon Int.

23 Oct Chinese Restaurant, Café.

24 Oct My Way Theatre.

25 Oct My Way Theatre.

26 Oct Small unit day trip to Paris for Parisian Scenes.

28 Oct WEEK FIVE – Hotel Room (Scene 75), Bathroom Int.

29 Oct Jubilee Street.

30 Oct Sid's Mum's.

31 Oct Wally's Gaff (scheduled but not shot due to actor indisposition).

1 Nov (My appointment book reads Paris and Dentist's; both are crossed out. However, a cast and crew party appears to have occurred starting 2100 hrs, at which I think I met Joe Strummer.)

2 Nov To New York; meet New York crew.

3 Nov Sunday. Sunny and warm. Arrange dredged-up cars in piles on New Jersey Docks. Alone with backhoe. Bliss.
4 Nov WEEK SIX – NY PRE-PRODUCTION
5 Nov Docks/Pizza/Taxi Scenes, New Jersey.
6 Nov F. Lee Bailey Office, Subway Train.
7 Nov Methadone Clinic Ext., Alphabet City, Max's Ext.'s.
8 Nov Max's office, 23rd St, Yankee Liquor, Ghetto St (#123A) (Video).
9 Nov Playland Ext., Times Square Ext., Fast Food Int., Rest.
11 Nov WEEK SEVEN – Chelsea Hotel Int.'s.
12 Nov Chelsea Lobby.
13 Nov To Los Angeles.
14–17 Nov (These days, amazingly, were free as we switched crews again and geared up for a 'new' shoot.)
18 Nov WEEK EIGHT – LA PRE-PRODUCTION
20 Nov Jail Cell, Prison.
21 Nov Granma's House.
22 Nov Mexican Bar, Granma Drive, Ext. GS Music Hall.
23 Nov Shoot video inserts.
24 Nov Location scout with Peter McCarthy – El Centro.
25 Nov WEEK NINE – Hospital, Methadone Clinic Int.
26 Nov Texas Clubs, Nursery (Starwood, W. Hollywood).
27 Nov Max's Int., Last Texas Club (Starwood).
28 Nov Fly to San Francisco.
29 Nov Shoot San Francisco scenes.
30 Nov Amtrak to LA with Gary.
1 Dec Crew to El Centro; Drive to Calexico with Roger and Dave; shoot Fried Chicken Int.
2 Dec WEEK TEN – Texas Bus Tour: El Centro, Brawley, Anza Borrego Desert. Return to Los Angeles.
3 Dec Miyako Ballroom (Universal City).
4 Dec Aeroplane Int.; Railroad Trax (Pacoima).
5 Dec Garbage Alley; Bowery Intro; Max's Office (downtown LA).
6 Dec Sunshine Inn (Sepulveda).
9 Dec WEEK ELEVEN – on stage at Cine-Pro, LA. Chelsea Hotel, Room 201 – (Scenes 147, 149, 153).
10 Dec Room 201 (Scene 155).
11 Dec Room 100 and Room 201 burn.
12 Dec Room 100 with Bowery.
13 Dec Room 100 & Wax Max's.
16 Dec WEEK TWELVE – Room 100 – Death scene.
17 Dec Room 100 after; Maida Vale.
18 Dec Wally's Gaff – La Brea stage (A final wrap party occurred that night).
19 Dec Leave Los Angeles for Mexico City, 2145 hrs on Western flight 456.

Post-production took place entirely in London, apart from some additional dialogue recording in Los Angeles, and John Cale's and Pray For Rain's music, which were recorded and produced in New York and San Francisco. The first cut was about three hours long; there was no need to shoot additional sequences. The sound mix was done at De Lane Lea in Soho; the mixer was Hugh Strain.

The title was changed, at the request of Zenith's Lawyers, to *Sid & Nancy*. It first played in the Quinzaine des Réalisateurs at Cannes in 1986.

Several actors involved in the film have admitted the three months of filming turned into a very drug-induced shoot. David Hayman, who played Malcolm McLaren, was part of this 'energising' experience:

> "Alex wanted a kind of heightened reality. I think it worked because there was a genuine madness and chaos to the performances which, at the time, I found very empowering. There was a lot of drugs around, from top to bottom. It wasn't actively encouraged but it certainly wasn't discouraged. I think it was important that we embodied the lifestyle of the people we were playing and, as a result, *Sid & Nancy* is, to this day, one of the most powerful anti-drug statements ever put on screen – far more effective than *Trainspotting*. Alex's film really shows the tragedy of people destroying their lives through excess. It just so happened that in the process of us portraying that, we too were excessive."

For the most part, Cox and Wool were blessed with good producers for *Sid & Nancy*. The only friction that developed on set seems to have been the result of Cox's unique way of working with actors. According to David Hayman, some had a tougher time than others:

> "Some found it hard to cope. Alex creates a chaos and then puts a control on it. His basic philosophy is to keep actors starved and naked in a cage all day, let them out once to be kicked, humiliated and abused in front of a camera and then throw them back in the cage again. That's a fairly individual way of approaching work and you have to take it tongue-in-cheek, but I remember by the time we were nearing the end of filming in LA, there were extraordinary scenes of some of the actors jumping into cabs for the airport so they could fly home a week before the end of the shoot. Eric Fellner had tried to talk them out of it but failed. They were all screaming they hated Alex and thought he was a fascist, so I chased after them and explained he was only creating the anarchy that enabled him to work.

> Some actors feed on the energy he creates, others reject it. It's also annoying that you can't really get to know Alex. He's a master of deflection. He puts up a smoke screen and talks in riddles. On the plus side, he does allow actors freedom once they're out of the cage. If an artist wants to do something radically different, Alex will shoot it – as long as they've also done their research. Other directors will just treat actors nicely but then put them in a straight jacket once they're in front of the camera. Nevertheless, I think the guys in the band had to put up with a lot, the long hours and so on. Maybe I enjoyed the shoot more because I wasn't part of the main focus of the film. As for Gary Oldman, I think it's a shame he doesn't really talk about *Sid & Nancy* much because that film made him. The film is a bench mark in the history of cinema, a real seminal movie."

Miguel Sandoval believes he was brought in for a few days on the Texas shoot because Cox needed a friendly face around:

> "It was obvious Alex was having real trouble with Gary Oldman and they weren't getting on at all. In fact, later on, after the film was released, Gary wrongly told the press he had directed his own performance as well as Chloe's because Alex was drunk and stoned all the time. That astounded me not just because it wasn't true but also because *Sid & Nancy* really put Gary on the map, and you'd think he'd give Alex at least some credit."

Sandoval's short time spent hanging around on the Texas tour bus resulted in one of the best comic scenes in the film. He is a record company executive who is proud to have written his own 'punky' song and tries to convince Johnny Rotten it could be the next Sex Pistols hit. To the horror of Rotten, he proceeds to sing the melodic chorus:

"I wanna job, I wanna job, I wanna good job,
I wanna job, I wanna job that pays.
I wanna job, I wanna job, I wanna real job,
One that satisfies my artistic needs."

"Alex put a wig on me, sat me next to Drew Schofield on the tour bus, stuck a camera in my face and told me to go for it. My part was all improvised and done in one take," recalls Sandoval.

Chloe Webb as Nancy Spungen.

›› Gary Oldman as Sid Vicious.

Interestingly, a behind-the-scenes documentary by Martin Turner could have given a rare insight into Cox's direction of actors but ended up more of a parody of 'making of' programmes. This was intentional and everyone who took part was in on the joke. The 45-minute film featured the key members of the cast talking with – and about – Alex Cox. As part of Turner's send-up, David Hayman was all set to meet the real Malcolm McLaren for a pretend shoot-out on a beach in Santa Monica. However, by this time, McLaren had seen some rough cuts of the film and hated what he saw. He refused to turn up for the 'documentary'. Nevertheless, Hayman says he still came out of the film with a lot of respect for McLaren:

> "He discovered and unleashed a hell of a lot of talent on the world and it was a real challenge to play him. I'd watched all the interviews with him to get the accent and his mannerisms and I tried to capture the essence of what McLaren's character and lifestyle was all about. My portrayal was never intended to be 'the truth'. Acting is the illusion of truth and I think Alex, Gary and all of us got the essence of what Sid and Nancy and the Sex Pistols were all about."

Sid & Nancy was a film in which Cox could once again use his interest in punk rock to comment on this movement that he saw as a rebellion against the social, economic and political climate of the time. Punk was a reaction against outdated society, and tried to promote forward movement. Particularly in Britain, the movement was a rebellion against the institution of the monarchy, the Queen of England having celebrated her 25th year of her reign in the 1977 Silver Jubilee celebration. The monarchy became a big issue because it was the foundation stone of a society that emphasised class differences. It was, and still is, a blatant example of how a system tolerates the unfairness of inherited status and wealth, while at the same time does little to help the poor. Most kids in British working class neighbourhoods left school with very limited prospects, doomed to become part of the British welfare system. With the only option of becoming like their parents, they had to find another way out.

Youthful rage and frustration could be expressed through music, fashion and a do-it-yourself attitude based on individuality and self-expression. The punk scene resisted commercialism, had little or no fashion sense, or at least a different fashion, again, with the emphasis on individualism. Punk was a powerful democratising force in the music industry, a real anti-movement in rock. It brought a new form and attitude to music, loved by those who were sick of the Seventies' hard rock and disco scenes with music that made no statements. Not everyone wanted to hear about sex, drugs, and rock and roll all the time. Both an artistic and political movement, for a brief time, before the advent of MTV, punk brought the means of production back to the music workers. Ironically, *Sid & Nancy* shows how Vicious and Spungen betrayed the punk movement.

» The original handwritten lyrics for the *Sid & Nancy* title song 'Love Kills' by Joe Strummer. He signs off "I hereby resign from showbiznis."

"Punk was supposed to be about rebellion and forward movement. When I was a student in Bristol, I saw a guy walking down the street wearing a jacket with the date, 1976, written on the back. It just seemed to me that it was very important that he'd done that. Punk was about taking control, making a difference and not being like one's forebears. But Sid essentially becomes like a rock dinosaur and retreats into a junkie pad and is constantly cadging money to pay for the heroin. That's not what the punk movement was supposed to be about. At the time, I had read the William Burroughs' book *Junkie* which I was intrigued by and, at a distance, it is a fascinating culture. But since then I have had friends who have become junkies and, close up, there is nothing really fascinating about it at all. They are tedious people who lie and, if they are poor, break into your house and steal all of your stuff. The hardest thing to deal with is a junkie couple because they reinforce each other's addictions. It is almost impossible for either of them to cease their addictions without splitting up.

"However, I also showed their story as a love story because, despicable though they were, in their own way they were in love. There was a certain value to that. Although I think I felt that more strongly then than I do now. I don't find it so romantic any more. It disappoints me that the punk culture became associated with the junkie culture, partly because of people like Sid and Nancy. But to me, it was nothing to do with punk. Heroin and coke were a betrayal of the punk culture, in just the same way as becoming hugely wealthy and living in a mansion would be a betrayal of the punk culture. Nevertheless, no matter how horrible you make the junkie culture look, there are always going to be certain people who are attracted to it.

"In fact, looking back, I think I was slightly guilty of tending to romanticise the junkie culture. Film-makers still do it. There's a scene in *Trainspotting* when they leave a body of a guy who has overdosed in the street with a five-pound note on him so that a taxi driver will take him to hospital. They wouldn't do that. It just wouldn't happen. And if a taxi driver did come along, why wouldn't he just take the fiver? What does he want a vomiting junkie in his taxi for? That seemed to me to

LOVE KILLS

ON THAT BUS THAT GOES TO MEXICO
A KILLER OFTEN FINDS A SWEET MEXICAN GIRL
YEAH 'BETCHA THOUGHT OF RUNNIN'
FOR A SMALL SHANTY TOWN IN A SOUTHERN WORLD

IN MISSIPPI - WE RUSH YOU TO THE ROPE
DOWN IN DIXIE YOU GO CRYING FOR DOPE
DOWN IN ALABAMMY WE LIKE HOME COOKED FARE
SO WE GONNA STRAP YOU TO THE FRYING CHAIR

I DONT KNOW WHAT LOVE IS
RIGHT NOW SOMETHING ELSE HAS GIVEN ME THE CHILLS
BUT IF MY HANDS ARE THE COLOUR OF BLOOD
THEN I CAN TELL YA, SURE I CAN TELL YA
LOVE KILLS LOVE KILLS

DID YA WANNA HEAR THE SIRENS
ALL THE SIRENS IN THE CITY HOWLING OUT YOUR NAME?
UP RIVER RIKER'S ISLAND GOT A POPULATION, BOY
THEY WONT CARE ABOUT YOUR FAME

BUT ON THE RIO GRANDE
- WE'LL TIE YOU TO A TREE
AND YOU CANT CALL YOUR LAYWERS
- COS THE WHOREHOUSE IS ASLEEP

YOU EVIL MOTHERFUCKER
- YOU CANT FUCK WITH ME
I'LL THROW YOU IN A CELL
- WITH THE BARRIO THREE

I hereby
Resign from
Showbizness
Joe Strummer

> be a romantic vision of it which, rather like some of *Sid & Nancy*, isn't really true.
>
> "All in all, I hope *Sid & Nancy* doesn't depict being a junkie in too positive a light; Gary and Chloe are great actors and there is a lot of truth to what they do. I am afraid we may have sentimentalised their characters' end."

Cox's film achieves great authenticity, charting Sid's introduction to the mayhem world of the Sex Pistols, his obsession with violence, his relationship with Nancy and their decline into heroin-induced paranoia. *Sid & Nancy* has been recognised as the definitive movie on the punk phenomenon, bringing the viewer as close as possible to understanding the ravaged pair. It's not necessary to like punk music to feel sympathy for the tortured, drug-addicted couple or to be carried away by Cox's ability to mine humour out of the most harrowing situations – drink, drugs and sometimes sex.

Nevertheless, there are inaccuracies. Cox shows the Pistols on their British tour, performing to a wild and adoring audience, whereas, in reality, away from the punk scene of bigger cities, the band were met more with a mix of bewilderment, animosity and even indifference. Cox is well aware of this and readily admits to trying to make the punk scene look adventurous and extraordinary:

> "I believe most of the stuff about Sid and Nancy is fairly accurate but the early stuff on the punk scene in London is very exaggerated. They didn't have a mosch pit or anything like that, even in London. The dancing would really have been just four or five guys pogoing and listlessly bouncing up and down. Early on in the British punk scene, it wasn't anything like the craziness that developed later on in LA and then in Britain. Also, in the recreation of Malcolm McLaren's publicity stunt with the Pistols on a boat on the River Thames, there are more police and more violence than there was in reality."

Despite the lack of marketing surveys done before the film was a 'go' project, after the film's completion a set of focus group responses were collated by the Sam Goldwyn Company. Those who attended preview screenings of *Sid & Nancy* in Los Angeles were able to make their views known before the films release. One viewer described Cox's film as "degrading and revolting. There was nothing anyone could relate to. The characters were so inhuman." Another, "I feel this film was totally evil", while another said "Makes me uncomfortable but doesn't answer any questions. Where is the character growth?" One of the members of the focus group felt that Americans "were depicted as ridiculous." Finally, another said, "the script is deplorable. The look of the

▲ J Rae Fox, Abbe Wool and Linda Burbank on the *Sid & Nancy* set, New Jersey, 1985.

film surprised me for its apparent amateurism. The choice of shots were [sic] totally boring – there were no dolly shots or anything even subtly soothing."

Luckily, the preview responses had no bearing on Cox's final cut but they do go to show why it is important not to have too much trust in previews or focus groups.

Sid & Nancy clearly wasn't going to be for all tastes. Pale-faced Gary Oldman gives a truly graphic and horrifying performance, in a story essentially about wasted lives and wasted talent. Oldman won Best Newcomer at the London Evening Standard Film Awards shortly after the film's release and the film was in many critics' top 10 films of that decade, both in America and Britain ("Gary Oldman and Chloe Webb are almost too good for comfort...I feel trapped in the hell of the characters they portray." *Sunday Express*). Oldman also performs his own vocals, as does the superb Drew Schofield, with former Sex Pistol Glen Matlock, who has recorded the old tracks again. Incidental music is provided by the Pogues, Pray for Rain and Joe Strummer. Despite much critical praise for the film, another certain person was not in agreement.

> "Johnny Rotten was shocked and horrified when he saw the film at a press screening, believing it to be a film made by evil people who did it only for the money without consulting him or seeking his advice. That's the official

▲ Abbe Wool, Dick Rude and Vicky Thomas at the *Sid & Nancy* opening night, Los Angeles.

Johnny Rotten version, as repeated in his autobiography. But the official Johnny Rotten biography version of events simply isn't true. I actually met him at the Mayflower hotel in New York when we had just finished casting.

"He certainly wasn't in favour of the project but we met and had a very nice time. We drank a lot, mostly Seabreezes (vodka and cranberry juice) with the idea that it was good for you because it contained cranberry juice! So we had drunk about 20 Seabreezes and were getting on very well. He agreed for me to have Drew Schofield, who we had just cast for the Johnny Rotten part, fly over to New York to meet with him. There was no problem with that as far as Lydon was concerned. He seemed quite happy.

"Drew is a great actor, but someone who doesn't like to leave home for very long. He still lives in Liverpool. So he flew over for the weekend. But bearing in mind Johnny and I had drank 20 Seabreezes in two hours, can you imagine the amount of alcohol he and Drew consumed over their 18 hours together? Suffice to say Drew remembers going out with Johnny, talking about the character and how Rotten wanted him to play the part as a scouser, while Drew is thinking he can't possibly do that and is trying to concentrate on listening to Rotten's accent so he can later copy it. But then everything goes black. Drew wakes up at JFK airport being carried on to the plane to go back to England, all his notes lost long ago and with no recollection of what they had talked about.

"After Johnny saw the film, I suppose he didn't like it. It was a story very close to him. Sid Vicious was, according to the official version, Johnny's closest friend. In those circumstances, I think it would be unlikely if somebody did make a film about your best friend's tragic death that you would be entirely impressed by the finished film.

"What was great about Johnny Rotten's response was that it helped the film. In the same way that the Sex Pistols had profited from their bad reputation, worldwide outrage and endless firings from record companies, we too profited from his spirited and lengthy tirades in the media. Although, when he later released his PIL record that was called Album or Cassette or CD, packaged just like the generically labelled goods in *Repo Man*, I thought that was him saying, "See, two can play at this game." I was really flattered by that, because I thought that Album was a really great album, my favourite PIL album.

"So I hope that, even if he doesn't remember the events as clearly as he might, a lot of his outrage was actually theatrical outrage and that he had a certain soft spot for us film-makers, because we had no intention of doing him wrong."

Although the sordid lives of Sid and Nancy may not usually be typical material for a movie romance, take away the drugs and the vomit and you are left with a very convincing love story. The romance is genuine. Before they met each other, neither of them really had anything but after they got together it seems they really did love each other unconditionally. After Nancy is rejected by Johnny Rotten, who declares sex 'boring', she latches on to Sid and eventually becomes absorbed by this guy who wants her for something more than sex and drugs.

Cox's black, quirky humour, throughout the first half of the film makes us, the viewers, really grow to like this couple. They don't care about anything or anyone except each other. And, above all else, before we see the horrors of drug addiction really kick in, we see how they have fun, endlessly. There is even a sense of childlike innocence to their ways as they run around like kids having pretend shoot-outs on a hotel roof.

On the surface, the lives of Sid and Nancy would seem to bear little relation to our own. But it is the organisation of fantasy that engages us and allows us to identify with characters like Sid and Johnny. Cox's ensemble of textual devices engage the viewer in fantasy, playing on wishes and desires present in our own lives. Viewers gain pleasure through seeing the two main characters disturb the boundaries. We get to confront their lifestyle and at the same time get to indulge in their behaviour. *Sid & Nancy* allows us, as spectators, the chance to play out our own fantasies of rage and anger. We can play around with these elements Cox has mixed together, bending his meanings to our own purposes. After all, when it comes down to it, Sid and Nancy are pure rebels and their lifestyles are rebellious acts against banal society and general tedium, which is why we enjoy see Sid shooting all the stuffed shirts in the theatre for the My Way video. Haven't we all, at some point, wanted to lash out in this essentially, straight, boring world.

Loud and adventurous, the pair became a walking disaster area, their appearance offering hope that there was more to popular music than airbrushed beauty and glossy videos. Pushing working class opinions into the mainstream, Sid and Nancy, early on, were part of a cultural force to be admired. But, in the end, they spoilt whatever they had for each other and degraded the punk culture by killing themselves with drugs.

In Cox's reconstruction of events, we see how they are each other's downfall. Nancy, an American groupie has arrived in London with little money and a severe drug addiction, and is a bad influence on Sid. He has never done hard drugs before meeting Nancy, but within a few days of meeting her, he is as dependent on heroin as she is. Then, within a year of Sid joining the Sex Pistols, his habit starts seriously to affect their performances. During the disastrous American tour, Johnny Rotten breaks up the band.

After recovering from his first overdose, Sid agrees to stay in New York with Nancy who takes on the role of his manager as they try to launch his solo career. They become a fun couple but with no real success. They wind up in the Chelsea Hotel after being rejected by Nancy's family, who are resigned to the fact she can never change her ways. They try to go straight, but with only each other to turn to, they never manage it. Their lives are reduced to endless amounts of drugs and TV. In the end, they give up. Nancy hounds Sid about ending their lives together, believing it to be the only way out of their living hell. Nine months after the demise of the Sex Pistols, Sid is arrested for stabbing Nancy to death. Whether it was a tragic accident that happened while the pair were too high to get help, no one will ever know, but the film indicates she goaded him to it.

Four months later, Sid died of a massive heroin overdose awaiting trial. Cox's film ends with an amazing fantasy sequence. As Sid dances with four little black kids on deserted wasteland, in his drugged-up brain, Nancy pulls up in a cab. He joins the fantasy by getting into the cab with her. Together, they ride off into the sunset, leaving the black kids boogying to hiphop, the next craze in music history.

Nancy and Sid
RIP

Chapter Five

Life after Sid

After work was completed on *Sid & Nancy*, Cox took the film to the Cannes Film Festival. It would be here that he would find the inspiration for his next film, *Straight to Hell*.

At the festival, Cox stayed in the same hotel as the producer, Eric Fellner, as well as Gary Oldman, Chloe Webb and other actors who had gone along to help promote the film. They had separate rooms but, according to Cox, his own room became a kind of boys' dorm because Strummer, Rude, Richmond *et al.* had no rooms! After spending the evening doing interviews with journalists eager to hear about his new film, Cox returned to his hotel to see an image that would stay with him:

> "I got in to find Joe Strummer, Dick Rude, my cameraman friend Tom Richmond all sitting round a table in the hot sun, looking absolutely awful! They were hungover, drinking endless cups of coffee and looking a real mess. They had slept in their clothes; they were dirty and sweaty and tired and the sun was beating down on them as they thought about beer and drank more coffee. Sara Sugarman was seated there, too, totally calm and looking like an angel."

This image formed the basis of *Straight to Hell*, which takes its title from a song by the Clash. It's a combination of the punk sensibility of Cox's first film, *Repo Man*, and a wildly anarchic spoof of the spaghetti westerns of Sergio Leone. Eric Fellner produced the film:

> "I remember all of us saying, "Fuck it. Let's just go and make a film. Why should we spend years writing it, financing and developing it?" There was also intense interest after the success of *Sid & Nancy* at Cannes and everyone wanted to be in business with Alex and me. We didn't have an official working partnership, but at that point I think we both felt we'd like to continue working together. You see more of that kind of working relationship today with people like Andrew McDonald and Danny Boyle, who have one little movie that becomes a hit and then create a producer–director partnership."

Above all, *Straight to Hell* is great fun with an improvisational air and some brilliantly camp dialogue. Filmed in Spain, Tom Richmond's photography mimics the spaghetti western style perfectly.

The plot concerns money. After a botched robbery, a band of thieves – surly Norwood (Sy Richardson), Willy (Dick Rude) and Simms (Joe Strummer) – rob a rank and head off into the desert. They make their getaway with Velma (Courtney Love), Norwood's girlfriend, who is pregnant with his child. In the middle of the desert, their Honda breaks down and the bumbling foursome take refuge in Blanco Town which is run by a murderous, incestuous clan of trigger-happy coffee addicts known as the MacMahons, played by the Pogues.

Fans of *Repo Man*, the hard-drinking Irish band had struck up a good relationship with Cox after he agreed to direct a video for their 1985 single *A Pair of Brown Eyes*. It was shot in London just before work began on *Sid & Nancy*. Much of the filming for the three-minute promo was done inside a tube train at Golder's Green station. The video features 'eyes' everywhere: inside a brown paper bag, on stickers plastered all over the train's windows and painted on the hand-grips. Eye-level adverts were replaced with portraits of Thatcher – her own beady eyes staring down. Passengers have bandages strapped around their eyes and headphones over their ears, Cox's statement being that people are letting government turn society into a police state. Brainless idiots wandering around with Walkmans, not seeming to care what politicians are going to dump on them next.

After the *Pair of Brown Eyes* video, the Pogues composed instrumental music for *Sid & Nancy*, before following Cox to Almería for their foray into acting.

The characters in *Straight to Hell* were written for the actors. Co-writer Dick Rude is excellent as Willy; he is a very interesting actor and laugh-out-loud funny in this film. It's surprising that with his obvious good looks, Rude didn't land more lead roles.

After her small role in *Sid & Nancy*, this was Courtney Love's first leading role. She is very impressive and her character, Velma, is like a tougher version of Nancy Spungeon – or, as Love described the part, "a white-trash pregnant bitch, some weird hillbilly from an incestuous background who's fascinated with charms and magic."

▲ Sara Sugerman, Alex Cox, Courtney Love.

However, after successfully reinventing herself, Love chooses not to talk much about the film. After praise for her performances in films such as Milos Forman's *The People vs. Larry Flynt*, she's cleaned up her image, ditched the grunge look and now looks and acts more like a 'traditional' movie star. In interviews for various TV programmes, including the American *Today Show*, she refused to answer questions about drug use, even walking off set when the interviewer persisted. Instead, Love has taken part in carefully orchestrated profiles in glossy magazines like Vogue, and appeared, on her best behaviour, at the 1997 Academy Awards. Just two years earlier, at a 1995 Oscars' party, a less polite Courtney Love bludgeoned the journalist Lynn Hirschberg with Quentin Tarantino's Oscar. She had annoyed Love by writing an article for Vanity Fair that mentioned her use of heroin during pregnancy. Reminders of the old Courtney didn't fit in with the new way she wanted to be perceived. She has even been hailed as a role model by the US magazine *Brandweek*, coming third in a list of Hollywood celebrities whose fashion sense is respected. The fact that Courtney Love was an

actress in Cox's films in the mid-Eighties, and looked completely different, is something she would rather people didn't know about.

The cast of *Straight to Hell* is also littered with an array of hip celebrity cameos from such punk luminaries as Elvis Costello (as a coffee-dispensing butler), Grace Jones, Jim Jarmusch and Dennis Hopper, whose name is the same as the German

Counter cultural cameos. Grace Jones and Dennis Hopper (above); Jim Jarmusch (right).

▲ "Cox was nuts on *Straight to Hell*." Kathy Burke with Xander Berkeley and Zander Schloss (centre).

industrial agent, IG Farben. Another highlight is the wickedly funny Kathy Burke as Sabrina. Burke followed Cox to Almería after her brief stint in *Sid & Nancy*: "It was great fun but the work was fucking stupid. Cox was nuts on *Straight to Hell*, a complete and utter egomaniac. But the pop stars thought it was great because the set was so anarchic..." After *Straight to Hell*, Cox asked Burke to join him in Nicaragua for his political allegory, *Walker*: "I thought I'd end up getting shot but Alex took me to a Mexican restaurant and persuaded me to go. I'm glad I did. It was a fantastic experience – meeting 14-year-old kids prepared to go out and die for their country."

Cox's strange hybrid of new-wave humour is present throughout, mixing reality and fantasy to create another insane world of weird dialogue and behaviour. There's an amazing shoot-'em-up finale, but one of the best scenes has to be when the local geeky hotdog seller (Zander Schloss) is forced to sing The Wiener Song at gunpoint. ("Let's make that Wiener kid sing his song! Wanna?") The MacMahons then throw vegetables at him and taunt him with the idea of shooting him. The Wiener Song is just one of the tracks on a top film soundtrack, with almost everyone in the film having a role in the music. One great performance is that of Fox Harris singing Delilah, accompanied by Elvis Costello. The Pogues produced the opening theme and an epic guitar-driven score is provided by Pray for Rain.

Cox was already preparing what would be his fourth film, *Walker*, when *Straight to*

Hell happened as quickly as it did. He chose to film *Straight to Hell* first so that it would prepare him for filming in Nicaragua. Both films were set in Spanish-speaking countries but *Walker* was a much bigger production, with added political tensions. *Straight to Hell* gave Cox a chance to practice his Spanish. By the time he had finished filming, he was proficient in the language and ready to head for Nicaragua and Mexico, to continue pre-production on *Walker*.

However, the development of *Straight to Hell* goes back to when Cox was still editing *Sid & Nancy* in London, and just before the infamous coffee-crazed vision at the Cannes Film Festival.

Cox organised a concert at The Fridge in Brixton, in support of the FSLN (Sandanista National Liberation Front) in Nicaragua. About 4000 people turned up on the night and half of them couldn't get in to the packed venue. The Pogues, Elvis Costello and Joe Strummer all played to a full house and raised a few thousand pounds for the Nicaragua Solidarity Campaign. Based on the concert's success, Eric Fellner came up with a grander scheme: since the public clearly loved the musicians and was sympathetic to the Nicaraguan cause, why not organise a rock 'n' roll tour of Nicaragua, involving the same people? With his experience in the music business, Fellner wanted put the finance together for the tour and tried to get a video deal to pay for it. In the meantime, Cox persuaded the said musicians to sign up for the Nicaragua Solidarity Tour in August 1986. All of them agreed. However, Fellner was finding it difficult to obtain funding because bands like The Pogues have families and many instruments. This would have cost a small fortune to transport them over to do the concerts. As the date approached, it became clear that no video company would fund the tour.

This put Cox in a very embarrassing position, having persuaded at least a dozen musicians to take the entire month of August off. Fellner's solution was to make a film instead. As he predicted, it was easier to raise a million dollars for a low-budget feature starring various musicians than to find $75 000 to film them playing in a revolutionary nation in the middle of a war.

Eventually, Cox wrote the script with Dick Rude, over three days, in a Los Angeles hotel. The film was made for Island Pictures, a division of the record company, and was shot over a period of just four weeks in August 1986.

DIARY OF ALEX COX – THE MAKING OF *STRAIGHT TO HELL*

We filmed in Almería, Spain, according to this approximate schedule:

1986

4 Aug	WEEK ONE. Gran Hotel, Almería, Ints and Exts.
5 Aug	City Outskirts, Benehadux, Ravine.
6 Aug	Pueblo Blanco, Tabernas Desert, Almería.
7–9 Aug	As above.
11 Aug	WEEK TWO. As above.
18 Aug	WEEK THREE. As above.
25 Aug	FINAL WEEK. As above.

The film was edited by David Martin, in Soho. The sound designer was Justin Krish. The original, four-day version was complete in December 1986. The editor, producer and I recut it to a three-day saga in March 1987.

The month in Spain wasn't an entirely easy ride. The funding Eric Fellner received from Island ran out half way through filming and he ended up financing the rest of the shoot on traveller's cheques and credit cards. This didn't cause too many problems because Cox was a hot property and people were confident *Straight to Hell* was going to be a success. At the time, Fellner wasn't concerned:

> "Everyone wanted to work with Alex. Dennis Hopper and Grace Jones had already signed up for cameos. Then we realised we needed two more cameos for a couple of GI characters who in just one scene. We approached Tim Robbins and John Cusack who said they were really excited about doing it. They were in the middle of shooting movies in Hollywood, being paid a million dollars each, but took a day off to come to Spain for no money to work with Alex. When they arrived on set, Alex turned round, looked at them and in his own

››Mister Big Shot! *Sid & Nancy* and *Straight to Hell* producer Eric Fellner has gone on to produce many of the highest grossing European features of the Nineties. *The Sunday Times* named him with his partner Tim Bevan, the most powerful men in British film history having signed a $600 million deal with Universal – the studio that blacklisted Alex Cox.

inimitable style announced, "They've got to shave their heads or else I'm not shooting them." As their jaws dropped, I tried to explain they couldn't go back to Hollywood to finish films, already in production, with shaved heads. "Fuck it then," said Alex. "I won't use them." So they went home. That is Alex Cox. I love him madly but he's also the most annoying person in the world. Once he's made a decision about something, you cannot change his mind whether there's logic to it or not. I admire that side to him, but as a producer working with a director, I hate it. That sort of thing started to happen a lot and I began to realise he always seems to like or need clearly to fixate on a negative. It's almost as if when he had that negative to hang on to, everything else could be great. He needed something to channel all his aggression towards, whether it was a person, a situation, a political statement or whatever. That would then free him up to put good work into everything else. Sometimes he would fixate on a

▼ "Let the Weiner kid sing his song!" Zander Schloss (right) with Sue Kiel.

▲ Before the make-over. Courtney Love on set in *Straight to Hell*.

member of the crew, sometimes it would be an actor. He's an intense director and used to refer to actors as 'talking props', so you can imagine what many actors thought of him. There were times when he pushed them further than they wanted to be pushed. Sometimes that created brilliance and other times it created resentment. He's smart and a very forceful character, but sometimes I think he dazzles himself and, as a result, loses his vision. It was always a challenge working with him, even if I didn't always agree on things – and it was always bloody hard work."

Straight to Hell opened in London and Dublin, on 12 June 1987, one day after the British General Election (Mrs Thatcher won). Its US opening was on 1 July, following a private screening for the Vicomte and Vicomtesse de Noailles at the Pic-Wik Drive-In, Studio City, Los Angeles.

At this point, Cox was only known for his two punk-inspired films, but *Straight to Hell* is a film that highlights his love of spaghetti westerns. A lot of critics didn't share his enthusiasm and attacked his homage.

Film critics weren't alone in giving *Straight to Hell* the thumbs down. According to Eric Fellner, the film destroyed his working relationship with Cox:

"While *Sid & Nancy* is a masterpiece, I think *Straight to*

Hell is just too anachronistic. The truth is, that film caused me a lot of pain. I'd never made a film before *Sid & Nancy*. We were fêted everywhere and then, suddenly, we went from this huge success to an unmitigated disaster where everyone was on my case trying to get their money back. It was a year of horror after the film was finished."

Depressed, Fellner pulled out of Cox's next film, *Walker*, and instead produced *Pascali's Island*, a period drama with Ben Kingsley, at the far extreme of *Sid & Nancy* and *Straight to Hell*:

"It was as if I had to cleanse myself of that period, even though I owe everything to Alex. Without him I would never have made *Sid & Nancy*, which was the most brilliant first film a producer could ever make."

Having gone their separate ways, Fellner moved into the mainstream. In 1991, with his partner, Tim Bevan, he revamped a production company called Working Title Films. At their London offices, corridors are lined with posters of films Fellner has been responsible for, including *Four Weddings and a Funeral*, *Elizabeth*, *Dead Man Walking* and

▼ Cox (second left) with the lead actors.

▲ Everyday activity in Blanco town.

Notting Hill. However, anyone entering Fellner's office can't miss the giant poster of *Sid & Nancy* that covers the wall behind his desk. He has by no means forgotten his time spent with Cox:

> "I'll never rule out working with Alex again but, at the moment, I feel he's a very specific film-maker, making films that interest him and not necessarily films that interest a substantial audience. I find myself in a difficult position because I'm a financier. I'm not in the art-house market any more, so its unlikely Alex and I will work together in the near future. If and when I'm more of a producer and less of a financier, maybe there'll be a time when, with the right script, we can come back together and do something again."

Cox doesn't regret making *Straight to Hell*. After the success of *Repo Man* and *Sid & Nancy*, he was offered big bucks to direct *The Three Amigos*. However, directing a few 'comedians' from the American TV show, *Saturday Night Live*, for a big Hollywood studio, wasn't the kind of experience he was looking for. Instead, he chose to concentrate on his own project. Compared with *The Three Amigos*, *Straight to Hell* is by far the funnier film.

Even at the time of release, Cox says he wasn't surprised by the critics' reaction:

> "My film was a genre-mixer and was slightly odd and before the cynical violence-fests of the Nineties, so maybe I should have made the film later on. If *Straight to Hell* had been released in the wake of films like *Reservoir Dogs* or *El Mariarchi*, when critics were comfortable with that mixture of bloodthirsty violence and humour, then it might have been more popular with the critics. So I think their reaction was regrettable but also inevitable. It was too grotesque for them."

Nevertheless, *Straight to Hell* did receive the Critics' Prize at the 1987 Madrid Festival. On the jury that year was a film-maker by the name of Sergio Leone: "I have been told about that and its great to think the old master really did see *Straight to Hell*!"

Cox is also a big admirer of the bleak, pessimistic Italian westerns directed by Sergio Corbucci. His 1969 film *The Big Silence* (*Il Grande Silenzio*) took place in the

▼ Strummer, Richardson and Rude in Cox's demented western.

snow. The mad plot, involving a mute gunfighter, ends with the bad guys winning absolutely. Corbucci's earlier work, *Django* (1966) was even more insane and set entirely in a sea of mud. *Django* was also very influential and spawned at least 30 sequels, including Giulio Questi's 1967 film, *Django Kill*, the main inspiration for Cox's *Straight to Hell*.

> "I had long wanted to make a spaghetti western, and *Walker* was taking time to put together. It's not often opportunities come up to make a film like *Straight to Hell*!
>
> "For me, the greatest pleasure of *Straight to Hell* was filming in that fantastic, surreal Andalucia landscape – the desert of *Lawrence of Arabia*, *The Good, The Bad and The Ugly* and *Figures in a Landscape* – films with extraordinary locations: the weird, ancient clay and sandstone and volcanic badlands, the huge triangular mountain of El Faro on the horizon. There is a certain beauty to being on location, to working in Spain, in Mexico, staying in white-walled towns, walking the streets at night, rising at dawn and working out in the desert till the last light of the sun is gone, which cannot be simply explained.
>
> "*Straight to Hell* was my homage to the Italian film director Giulio Questi, and his film *Django Kill* (1967). Questi directed another bizarre film *A Curious Way To Love*, also in 1967, about a power struggle, for control of a chicken ranch, between the sadistic chicken breeder, his dominatrix wife and her murderously inclined niece. Like *Django Kill*, a complicated plot involving money, power, grotesque killings (the chicken breeder falls into his chicken food machinery and is mangled to death) and a backdrop of brooding, menacing sex.
>
> "*Django Kill* is a very edited film! There are many quick cuts and obscure flashbacks – one of the shots is cut in upside down – this was the late Sixties, where flashy editing was king, and strange, acid-type dream sequences were increasingly popular. It starts with a dream-like sequence in which a hand and arm emerge outstretched from a grave: a reference to Buñuel's *Los Olvidados* – and a shot which Peckinpah also borrowed

▲ Tom Richmond, cinematographer, and Alex Cox, director decide which way the camera should point on the set of *Straight to Hell*.

for *Bring Me the Head of Alfredo Garcia*.

"It is a gothic western like the celebrated *Johnny Guitar*. As in Nicholas Ray's film, the characters are dressed in elaborate, uniform-type costumes. The bandits dress in rags; the soldiers they massacre are clad in dusty, bloodstained blue; the townspeople look like refugees from a bad version of *Dracula* (Jess Franco's); outside town lives a mad homosexual rancher, Zorro (no resemblance to Antonio Banderas or Douglas Fairbanks), who wears a white suit while his men dress in black mariachi uniforms.

"Most of the characters in the film are mad: the bandits who laugh as they murder their enemies and then their friends; the townspeople who conceal horrible secrets and will do anything for money; the wife whom the storekeeper keeps locked up, for fear she will set the house on fire (she does!); the crazed Zorro who converses with his parrot (the parrot talks

▲ Not enough coffee? Sara Sugarman looks on.

back), tortures people with crucifixion and an ordeal involving rats and bats.

"It is also rather a violent film. Though lacking the exploding blood of *The Wild Bunch*, *Soldier Blue* and many recent films, *Django Kill* is relentless in the cruelty of its characters, the delight they take in acts of mayhem, and the general atmosphere of bizarreness. The original version, screened in Italy, was called *E Se Sel Vivo Spara* (*If You Live, Shoot!*)

"The plot is more-or-less as follows: Django and his gang of Mexicans join up with Oaks' gringo gang to rob a US Army detachment escorting a 'Wells, Fargo' covered wagon carrying gold (pure spaghetti western fantasy – 'Wells, Fargo' didn't operate covered wagons and the Army didn't provide them with escorts). They massacre the soldiers (who are having a very gay splashing session in a river). Oaks double-crosses Django and murders the Mexicans, forcing them to dig

▲ Joe Strummer (Simms), Sy Richardson (Norwood) and Dick Rude (Willy) in *Straight to Hell*.

their own graves. Django is the only survivor. He is cared for by two mystic Indians, who believe he can tell them about the afterlife. Django manufactures bullets out of gold, and tracks Oaks to an inhospitable town called 'The Unhappy Place' (the location is the set of *A Fistful of Dollars*, a western town built in Colmenar outside Madrid). There he finds that Hagerman, a storekeeper, and Tembler, a hotelier, have inspired the townsfolk to shoot and lynch the bandits. Only Oaks remains alive.

"Django signs up to kill Oaks in a darkened warehouse, but Django is captured and tortured by Zorro, and reveals the gold's location. Zorro's men race to the cemetery and dig up the graves (another spaghetti western scene, since Leone's *The Good, The Bad and The Ugly* and Sergio Corbucci's *Hellbenders*). But the gold is no longer in the coffin, since Hagerman has hidden it in an upstairs closet in his home. Hagerman

A STORY OF BLOOD, MONEY, COFFEE, GUNS AND SEXUAL TENSION.
STRAIGHT
TO
HELL
ISLAND PICTURES Present An INITIAL PICTURES PRODUCTION
Of a COMMIES FROM MARS FILM "STRAIGHT TO HELL"
Starring
SY RICHARDSON · JOE STRUMMER · DICK RUDE
and COURTNEY LOVE
With Special Appearances by THE POGUES · ELVIS COSTELLO
DENNIS HOPPER · GRACE JONES · EDWARD TUDOR-POLE
and JIM JARMUSCH
Music by THE POGUES · PRAY FOR RAIN
Director of Photography TOM RICHMOND
Production Design ANDREW McALPINE
Editor DAVID MARTIN
Written by DICK RUDE and ALEX COX
Executive Producers CARY BROKAW, SCOTT MILLANEY
Producer ERIC FELLNER · Director ALEX COX
International distribution J & M Entertainment

▲ Are you a MacMahon or a mouse? The Pogues as the coffee-addicted clan.

murders Tembler and his wife; his house is set on fire by his own mad wife. Attempting to retrieve the gold from the closet, Hagerman is blinded by the molten gold. Django and the townspeople watch as Hagerman staggers about, dying and covered in melted gold, inside the burning house.

"Next morning, Django rides off, pausing to watch his two kids making distorted faces at each other, each one shouting, "I'm uglier than you!"

"*Django Kill* is one of thirty-one (!) sequels to *Django*, which was directed by Corbucci in 1966. Thomas Milian's character has little in common with Franco Nero's in the earlier film. It seems the copyright laws in Italy were very lax in the Sixties and Seventies, hence the many films featuring Django, Ringo, Trinity, Sartana and their friends. Many of these movies were very bad; some were very good; I have a particular fondness for *Django Kill*, since it is so extreme in every way – its costumes. its sets, its characters, its mad plot, its manic editing. It is one of the handful of great Italian westerns, along with *For a Few Dollars More*, *Once Upon a Time in the West*,

▲ Second assistant director, James O'Brien with young Nicaraguan actors.

Hellbenders, *Quien Sabe?* and *Big Silence*.

So therefore, if *Straight to Hell* is somewhat incomprehensible, it is only because it follows the demented and unclear structure of his film, which is so weird that there are even shots in there upside down. *Straight to Hell* could have been even stranger but Dick and I changed the script a lot during filming when we realised that our original script was difficult for people to understand unless they were actually obsessed with certain obscure spaghetti westerns.

While *Straight to Hell* was still in production, Cox was already very much involved in his next project, *Walker*. Lorenzo O'Brien, the producer, was already in Nicaragua, putting it all together. Initial funding from Martin Bedford, in London, and Edward Pressman, in the States, was already taken care of. So, as soon as the mad western was completed, Cox immediately embarked on what would be his most overtly political film to date. *Walker* was funded by Universal Studios at a cost of $5.8 million and was the biggest budget Cox had ever had.

Only Alex Cox could translate the absurd notion of an American becoming the President of Nicaragua. Cox once again takes his anarchic approach, this time to an astonishing piece of American history. *Walker* is a true story and Cox's film is a new-wave epic. William Walker was an American, a Tennessee-born adventurer, who abandoned brilliant careers in law, politics, journalism and medicine to become a soldier of fortune. His strong belief in manifest destiny led him to install himself as the President of Nicaragua in the mid-nineteenth century, with the view that America has a moral right to 'protect our neighbours from oppression'. With the financial backing of tycoon Cornelius Vanderbilt, Walker led a mercenary band of 58 men to Nicaragua in 1855. Against all odds, he made the civil-war-torn nation safe for Vanderbilt's steamships. Walker originally pledged to liberate Nicaragua for democracy but his real intention was to take over the country and annex it to the US. He didn't achieve this but did rule the tiny nation with an increasingly heavy hand for two years, until being kicked out by the end of 1857 after an astounding coalition of all five Central American nations. When he attempted a comeback, he was executed in 1860 by a Honduran firing squad. Cox's film tells the story of this short reign; two years of bloody tyranny.

As William Walker, authoritative Ed Harris lends great depth to the role at times, for example when Walker deals with his strong-willed deaf fiancée Ellen (played by Academy Award winner Marlee Matlin) who dies early on. Walker then becomes fatally twisted after her premature death. He boldly struts into battle, ahead of his renegade soldiers, as bullets whiz harmlessly past.

The rest of the cast include Cox stalwarts Miguel Sandoval, Xander Berkeley, Sy Richardson and Peter Boyle as Vanderbilt. Boyle was brought in after the original shoot when Universal agreed to fund some extra scenes in return for the acquisition of the foreign rights to the film. Rather than return to Nicaragua, the Vanderbilt scenes were

« *Walker* location scout, Granada, Nicaragua, 1986.

›› Cox location scouting for *Walker* in Durango.

shot in Tucson, Arizona. This resulted in the addition of the brilliantly over-the-top cameo from Peter Boyle:

> "I was happy to help Alex but I kept asking him if he'd created this guy, William Walker. I found the story so incredible. But one of the strangest things about the

US at that time was that people didn't get passionate about the situation in Nicaragua. The media spun it in a certain way which meant people didn't get what was going on there."

In terms of style, *Walker* was influenced by the films of Sam Peckinpah and Akira Kurosawa. Peckinpah was an American director who came out of television in the Fifties. Then, in 1969, he showed us what it was really like to get shot. In *The Wild Bunch*, we live that experience in painful slow-motion, in sequences that last as long as seven minutes. Bullets come from nowhere in a world based around human evil. Cox was influenced by the depiction of violence in *The Wild Bunch* and has a similar dark view of human nature, seeing Peckinpah's film as an allegory of America's involvement in a genocidal war in Vietnam, where outlaws and troops fought to produce the largest civilian 'body count' since World War II.

"There have been so many bloodthirsty adventure films made in the last 30 years that one tends to forget what a shock wave *The Wild Bunch* made when it came out in 1969. It was both condemned as violent pornography and lauded. At least one journalist – Alexander Cockburn – was so incensed that he got into a fist-fight in the cinema. In retrospect, *The Wild Bunch*, with its random cruelty, its senseless massacres, high-tech killing and gangsters dressed as US soldiers taking hostages and murdering old ladies – seems to be an early feature about Vietnam.

"Peckinpah is the kind of director that guys like. You don't find that many women interested in his meandering stories of embittered gunslingers brooding about betrayal and revenge. Yet, he was a man of contradictions too, and made one of the few westerns with a female protagonist – *The Ballad of Cable Hogue*. He hated studios: he took insane delight in torturing producers and was regularly fired during the editing of his films. Yet at the same time, he was repeatedly drawn to Tinseltown, and ended his days not like his mentor, John Huston, on a beach in Mexico, but in a broken-down trailer park in LA.

"Rumour has it that at the very end the great director brooded that his last completed work was a Julian Lennon video. A fitting fate, perhaps, for the great chronicler of men betrayed. Yet Peckinpah left behind more than a couple of pop promos. In addition to his westerns, Peckinpah's legacy includes *Straw Dogs*, a very odd film about holidaymakers in Cornwall, *Bring Me the Head of Alfredo Garcia*, the story of a severed head worth a million dollars, and *Junior Bonner*, Peckinpah's non-violent musing on the passing of the mythic West and the impossibility of honour in the contemporary world.

"My own film, *Walker*, is a Peckinpah film until a certain point. From the point of the battle where Walker's gang get trapped in the town, and particularly the battle at the end, the film is influenced mostly by Kurosawa's *Ran* (1985). I even had a tape of *Ran* on set in Nicaragua and must have watched it about 50 times. To make a film like that near the end of your career is astonishing. Akira Kurosawa is the greatest of all film directors. In some of his films – *Ikiru*, for example, or *Rashomon* – good triumphs in a compromised and temporary sort of way. In others – *Yojimbo*, *The Throne of Blood* and *Ran* – all notions of good and evil are meaningless; everybody's bad. If you win, it's just through concentration, cleverness or strength.

"A few years before he died, before a recent Oscars ceremony, various Americans tried to get Kurosawa to agree to be presented with an honorary Oscar for his services to film. The great man quickly put them in their place. On worldwide television, he announced that the Academy Awards were self-congratulatory bullshit, said that he was ashamed at how little he had learned in 50 years of film-making and that he would have to keep working until he died, in the hope that he would one day get it right."

In the final battle scene in *Walker*, Cox achieves the Kurosawa-style epic qualities by having almost no sound effects at all. Instead, we hear the warm, Spanish-music soundtrack which was composed by Joe Strummer with Zander Schloss. Schloss was leader of the Juicy Bananas back in *Repo Man* days, played with Pray For Rain on *Sid & Nancy*, sang the Weiner Song in *Straight to Hell* and is now the eminence grise of the Low and Sweet Orchestra in Los Angeles. The score is reminiscent of Bob Dylan's score for *Pat Garrett and Billy the Kid*, which contains 'Knocking On Heaven's Door', a song which Dylan wrote with Rudy Wurlitzer, screenwriter of both *Pat Garrett and*

Billy the Kid and Cox's *Walker*. Wurlitzer was fascinated enough by the story of William Walker to agree to write the screenplay:

▲ Cinematographer, David Bridges.

> "Walker is about obsessive power, how authority is achieved and then what happens after power is lost. It's about what that state of mind is when power is lost, and with William Walker, like Billy the Kid, that state is death."

Cox had been introduced to Rudy Wurlitzer by Harry Dean Stanton, during a film festival in Rotterdam, where *Repo Man* was playing.

> "I had seen Peckinpah's *Pat Garrett and Billy the Kid* and was fascinated by the idea within the film that both of these guys, Pat Garrett and Billy the Kid, make themselves celebrities by climbing up a pile of corpses. The film ends with all of their friends and associates dead, lying by the wayside, so the two of them can engage in their final duel. Even not knowing anything about Rudy Wurlitzer, having only seen this film as well

as *Two-Lane Blacktop*, it was very clear to me what Rudy was trying to say in his script. It is the idea that our society is based on death. Death and fame and power are all the same thing, and those who seek power and fame and glory are really seeking their own death, but are blind to it. Society is like a grim pile of corpses with a couple of monkeys on top, waving skulls.

"Later, I discovered that Rudy is a Buddhist and that those ideas are somewhat Buddhist notions. Death is part of life, and the inability to realise that creates mad fantasies that people engage in, which was the fantasy that William Walker engaged in as well. Walker led an army of guys to their deaths in Nicaragua, causing untold other deaths and murders and ruin. Really, all he was doing was seeking his own demise but could never find it. He was lucky; the great man of history who didn't get killed until way past his due date. So, in dealing with these themes, I knew Rudy was the man I needed to write the screenplay for *Walker*.

"I had been to Nicaragua in 1984 when there was the first legitimate, democratic election. The Sandinistas won. All the guys from the European parliament were there and declared it a clean election. At the time, there was a lot of support, in Britain and all over the world, for the Sandanistas. Oxfam produced a report called Nicaragua – the Threat of a Good Example? which concluded that the Sandanistas were an example to all of Latin America and all of the Third World of what a decent socialist government could achieve through the redistribution of wealth. Having won a revolutionary war in 1979, the Sandanistas had now won a perfectly legitimate democratic election in 1984. This really pissed off the Americans, who became determined to destroy that government, even if it meant destroying all of Central America in the process.

"On election day, since Managua was packed with journalists and election people, Peter McCarthy and I stayed in much preferable cities of Granada and León. We found ourselves in a hotel bar in León because it was the only place you could get a drink. They close most of the bars because on voting day you're meant to

▲ Ed Harris as Walker and Marlee Matlin as Ellen Martin.

be sober and serious! We met a couple of Sandinista soldiers at the hotel. They had been invalided out of the Army – wounded in combat with the Contras; one had shrapnel in his stomach, the other, had lost an eye. After a few drinks and after we had told them that we were film-makers, they immediately suggested we make a film in their country. So I start coming out with the usual lines to put people off the idea and how expensive the process is. But this soldier says "No. That's not true. You guys come from America, the land of money. You can go back to the States and get some money and come back here and make a film." I stopped and thought about this and knew that what he had said was really true.

"At the time, a bad film had been made called *Under Fire*, about how American journalists supposedly won the revolution for the Sandanistas. Although I wanted to make a film in Nicaragua, I didn't want to tell the story of a good white American journalist who goes and saves everybody. So I put a different slant on those political themes."

DIARY OF ALEX COX
THE MAKING OF *WALKER*

1984

3 Nov Back to Hotel Europa in León for poker and 100 000 beers. Our driver, Marciano, is a Somocista who hates the Sandinistas because five years ago the Cordoba was worth more and he had better clothes. He wants to go to the USA.

4 Nov Election Day. Short lines, many polling places, red thumbs on all the voters... Amble to the railway station... The train from Chinandega pulls in – one little diesel loco with three open coach/boxcars with bench seats facing in – no glass windows – people on roof... Fat woman: "I was a prostitute under Somosa. Now I am a Sandinista. Come." Not many red thumbs here. Back at hotel we meet two Compas (Sandinista soldiers). Both were wounded in a Contra attack in Murra. Their friend was killed there yesterday. One of them is in his first year of college. The other is still in high school. They are reading *La Prensa* – "All lies, but it proves we have a free press." Both have red thumbs. Voting age is 16; army is 17. As they're both seriously wounded (high school boy blinded in one eye by shrapnel), they don't have to return to the front. "But if there's an invasion, I'll go back anyway..." "If there wasn't a war, I'd like to be an agronomist..." They say their fight is harder because they take prisoners; the Contras torture/murder any soldiers or militiamen they capture. Also, they say the Contras can retreat into Honduras and the Nicaraguans cannot follow them.

They have no fear of a Contra victory. "They are still few in number, and not getting stronger."

"Mercenaries who run away."

The Contras have no popular support. The great fear everywhere, they young men say, is of a US invasion, from Honduras and Costa Rica. Every day the US invades Nicaraguan airspace...

One Compa asks if we will come back to Nicaragua to make a film. I say "espero" but it costs a lot of money. He is not impressed. "Si tu es intelligente..."

1985	
21 Dec	Western 456 arrives Mexico City 0420 hrs. Connects with AeroNica 527 to Managua; meet Lorenzo O'Brien, the producer of *Walker*, and Cecilia Montiel, the Art Director.
22 Dec	Scout San Jacinto, Old León, El Diamante, Realejo, Corinto, León.
23 Dec	Depart León; meet IMCINE in Manague.
24 Dec	Scout Rivas, San Juan del Sur (stay at Pension #28).
25 Dec	Scout La Marseilla, Diriambo, Pochomil.
26 Dec	Scout Granada.
27 Dec	Scout Lake Nicaragua islands by boat: Coyotepe, Fortoutside, Masaya.
31 Dec	0930 AeroNica flight 528 to Mexico City 1300 Pan Am flight 498 to Miami 1800 Pan Am flight 98 to London
1987	
12 Mar	Forced march of all the actors (except Parker French) led by Ed Harris.
14 Mar	FIRST DAY OF SHOOTING – Realejo.
16 Mar	WEEK ONE.
23 Mar	WEEK TWO.
30 Mar	WEEK THREE.
6 April	WEEK FOUR.
13 April	WEEK FIVE.
20 April	WEEK SIX.
27 April	WEEK SEVEN.
4 May	WEEK EIGHT.
11 May	WEEK NINE.

On the last day of production, Dave Bridges gave me the First Unit slate, which reads: Scene 83, Slate 588, Take 1 – a combination of US (scene #) and English (slate #) styles.

In other words, the First Unit made a total of 588 different shots; I'd guess the Second Unit, directed by Miguel Sandoval, made about a hundred more. So maybe 700 different shots (often with several takes of each) were available to us during cutting.

Carlos Puente and I edited *Walker* for eight weeks in Granada, Nicaragua. Joe Strummer stayed, too, working on the score.

On 13 July we made a full-coat protection master of the cutting copy in Mexico City (the negative was in London). The next day we took the film to the US, to begin sound work with Richard Beggs, in San Francisco.

On 14 and 15 August we shot two additional sequences at Old Tucson, Arizona – Walker meets Vanderbilt beside the train and sees the ghost of Ellen Martin; Vanderbilt humiliates Garrison and Morgan. Dave Bridges was again the cameraman; Tom Richmond shot Second Unit.

On 1 September, we viewed the film in San Francisco with Rudy and Ed; discussed a narration with Ed; Rudy went to work writing additional scenes.

▲ An American for President of Nicaragua? Ed Harris as William Walker.

On 6 September, we screened the film for Universal and requested money for additional shooting. Universal declined our request on 10 September. Lorenzo and I went ahead anyway and filmed additional sequences under the 1st Street Bridge on the night of 19 September – Debbie Diaz' birthday.

We recorded Ed's narration on 22 September.

The MPAA screened the film (presumably a tape) on 21 October, and declared that it would either receive an R or an X rating. No changes were made – it received an R.

Joe recorded his music in San Francisco, delivering the last track 'Remix Brooding #6' on 23 October. That day we left for the Zoetrope Winery Mix Room in Napa Valley, CA.

We mixed with Richard from 24 October to 3 November and screened the first married answer print at Deluxe in Los Angeles on 6 November.

The film opened on 4 December in eight American cities, after a benefit for MADRE in New York on 30 November.

It screened in Mexico at Churubusco Studios on 11 December and at the Havana Film Festival on 17 December.

I spent Christmas on the Wirral, and, on 30 December, saw *The Revenger's Tragedy* at the Stratford RSC.

Walker played at the Berlin Film Festival on 17 February 1988, two days after the death of Nora Astorga, former Sandinista Attorney General, of cancer.

Cox had made political statements in his work before he made *Walker*, for example, the hostility towards consumer culture in *Repo Man*. There is also a political aspect to *Sid & Nancy* which can be seen when Sy Richardson's character, the caseworker in the methadone clinic, tells the pair, "You've no right to be strung out on that stuff. You could be selling healthy anarchy." Cox was obviously suggesting the punk movement was, to some extent, a wasted historical opportunity. In this speech, Sy's character also talks about the Vietnam war being partially a cover for the American take-over of the heroin trade and how the Pentagon was bringing back, along with the bodies of the American dead, massive amounts of heroin into the US: "Smack is the great controller," he says, "It keeps people stupid when they could be smart." In fact, it is fair to say that most recent American administrations, including Truman, Reagan and Bush, made sure to open drug trafficking routes for illegal narcotics, under the cover of anti-communism. A Terrorism, Narcotics and International Relations Sub-committee, headed by Senator John Kerry, concluded that the CIA's war against the Sandanistas was substantially funded by drugs: "...it is clear that [the Contras] knowingly received financial and material assistance from drug traffickers...In each case, one or another agency of the US government had information about the involvement...Indeed, US policy-makers were not immune to the idea that drug money was a perfect solution to the Contras' funding problems." Of course, the US is one of the largest consumers of illegal drugs in the world, with around twenty million addicts.

Walker is Cox's most overtly political film. It was made in 1987, in the middle of the US-sponsored terrorist war against the FSLN and the Nicaraguan people. In his book, *The CIA: A Forgotten History* (1986), the CIA historian William Blum reveals that during President Reagan's first term alone, "the CIA-led, trained and funded Contra terrorists murdered 8000 Nicaraguan civilians" (p334). Later, around 20 000 civilians in El Salvador were murdered by American-trained death squads (US 'security forces' funded with $523 million in American 'aid'). The British government, under Thatcher at the time, supported American 'objectives' in Central America, which included those murders of thousands of innocent Nicaraguans. Foreign Secretary Geoffrey Howe 'absolutely endorsed' such terrorism. The use of force and illegal economic warfare against Nicaragua was deemed necessary so as to uphold and strengthen the force of democracy in an area threatened with a communist take-over. In fact, after popular democracy, health and education under Salvador Allende and the Sandanistas had later been shown as obviously successful, these achievements were suppressed with hardly any media coverage, compared with the earlier constant stream of press support for the American terrorist army, the Contra.

Cox's intention was to spend as many American dollars as possible in Nicaragua, in protest against the American government's outrageous aggression against a sovereign nation. To understand the present and the future, one needs to know the past, and Cox made sure of that. He made it clear that the film wasn't just an historical account of events that took place between 1853 and 1855, but also about current events.

Rudy Wurlitzer had already written a variety of scripts based around the nineteenth century, dealing with the notion of open country with a frontier mentality, both in terms of space and time. But *Walker* required something a little different, so Cox took Wurlitzer's script, imposed various contemporary images and took it into a surreal past–future domain.

Cox re-tells the story of the 1855 bloody and violent invasion of Nicaragua with great authenticity, yet populates this world with a variety of twentieth-century anachronisms (tape recorders, copies of Newsweek, personal computers and helicopters) as a reminder to viewers of America's continued interference with the Central American country. However, because these anachronisms aren't introduced until halfway into the film, the audience are simply not prepared for them. Cox now admits having them in from the start would have made the film a more unified piece:

> "In the very opening scene, when Walker tries to take over Mexico and fails, it should have ended with a Mexican bus driving through. Also, when Vanderbilt meets Walker in the desert, he should have been talking on a cellular phone! It was directorial error on my part not to have had the anachronisms in from the start."

Nevertheless, *Walker* still says more about real modern politics than any of the recent spate of Hollywood movies set in the White House. Cox was saying that nothing had changed since the Immortals took Nicaragua from its natives in 1855; Nicaragua was still owned by the US. William Walker's actions still have effects on US policy to this day. Not surprisingly, at the time of its release, Cox's film wasn't well received by the official media of a superpower engaged in a genocidal war. Universal was expecting the political aspect of the film but what caught them off guard was the anarchic tone. It wasn't a liberal interpretation. It exposes Walker as a man who conveniently forgot his liberal opinions, attempting himself to institute slavery just before his own demise. He is presented as someone who betrayed his allies, switching from liberator to dictator after becoming increasingly obsessed with power and glory.

One of Hollywood's liberals, Robert Redford, announced he would direct and star in his own film about William Walker, to set the record straight. He never did.

Walker deals with the idea that democracy is being destroyed as the US feels it must expand until it fills the whole American continent. Writer, Rudy Wurlitizer, recalls the change from the early days of the project, "when there was great energy because the producer, Ed Pressman, left us alone so the process was loose and free," to the time when the marketing people and studio executives came in:

"The Hollywood establishment is very liberal and they got really fucked up about the humour in Alex's film. It was very alienating to them. They thought it was too radical, but of course it's those elements that make the film great. Nowadays, studios always seem to want scripts that are too episodic with very constructed plots and traditional payoffs. Alex is a real artist. He's too pure and free to side with the money people, so instead he consistently ends up going to war with the powers that be. That takes great courage and the fact he can continue to work is very inspiring."

With a limited theatrical release, *Walker* failed to make an impact at the box office. Miguel Sandoval, who played Parker French in the film, believes it would have met with more success if Universal had bothered to get behind the project:

"I think the studio really wanted to screw Alex and the film because he had alienated them so much by just doing what he wanted. It wasn't Alex's fault that he had to direct a film that was way under-budgeted. We were up to our knees in pig shit, trying to shoot the battle scenes when the 'executives' would turn up in their tennis visors and polo shirts. Each time we looked at them, they'd have different coloured shirts on. They weren't used to the heat and were actually changing clothes every hour! On the way back to our bus, we were talking passionately about what shots we had and what we needed to do the next day, and these bond company guys came running up saying, "Alex, can we speak to you?" At which point Alex turned around and simply said, "Get away from me or I'll kill you." I think Universal reacted to Alex by deciding to just put up with one loss-making film, as long as they made sure he never worked in Hollywood again."

Nevertheless, *Walker* was a major turning point in Cox's career:

"I felt that my first three films could have been directed by anybody. The originality was in the screenplays rather than in the execution. I remember that before we started work on *Walker* I wrote myself a note

One of the key battle scenes
à la Kurosawa's *Ran*.

> saying that I really should try and do something that had the same level of originality as my student film and try to get out of the formulaic way of making films where you inter-cut two close-ups and Bob's your uncle!"

This point of view, coupled with the political comment, explains the use of twentieth-century anachronisms. It also explains one very long *plano secuencia* when William Walker and his men are trapped in a funeral parlour in Granada, a way of filming that Cox would develop later. This battle scene isn't shot in the conventional way. Instead, Cox shoots it all in one long single camera shot and it is certainly one of the best sequences in the film. He had wanted to do more of these sequences but because of mounting pressure from the studio, he thought it best to just get the film finished before the boom fell. However, this organic style would become a rule of thumb for Cox's films in the future.

Immediately after *Walker*, Cox was definitively blacklisted by the American studios and clearly was not going to get any sort of a 'normal' job in the US. His career wasn't about to follow the trajectory of the English film-maker who goes to work in Hollywood. He had begun his film career in Los Angeles with his student film and *Repo Man* and ended it there with *Walker*. As a result, in the following few years, Cox found it very difficult to find money to make films.

Having been rejected by Hollywood, Cox and Lorenzo O'Brien were made Honorary Citizens of Tucson, Arizona, for their work on *Walker*. Cox was already in development with Tristar Pictures to make a film on the bubble-gum card series Mars Attacks. He had already written two drafts of the screenplay, but after the hostile reaction to *Walker* in America, Tristar didn't want to know Cox. After all, he had spent many millions of American dollars, belonging to a capitalist American studio, to make a pro-Communist film. Naughty boy.

Tristar replaced Cox with another writer, novelist Martin Amis. He had never written a screenplay before and ended up delivering it very late. The studio didn't like what he had submitted and Amis then wrote an article in the New Yorker ridiculing the studio executives who had employed him. The entire project was cancelled.

Finding himself to be on a list of banned directors at various studios in Hollywood, Cox then spent a year in Tucson preparing a film called *Body Parts*, again written by Rudy Wurlitzer, about the alleged trade in infant body parts for transplant purposes in Latin America. The script was written with Harry Dean Stanton in mind but, at the last minute, he pulled out and so the money didn't appear. The film was almost made a few months later, with Rip Torn and Rosie Perez playing the leads. Once again, one of the backers pulled out at the appointed hour. The film never happened.

Cox also began writing with his current partner Tod Davies and, in 1988, they both helped out Cox's old *Straight to Hell* pal Dennis Hopper, who hired them to rewrite the script for a film he planned to direct called *Backtrack*. Cox and Davies had met

The membership card that Cox snatches and tried to rip up in front of Hopper's face.

when they were both students at UCLA but have since formed a long-term writing partnership. Cox stayed with Davies at the Hopper mansion in California while they worked on the script for *Backtrack*. At the time, Hopper was directing Robert Duvall and Sean Penn in *Colors*, a violent film about the intense gang warfare in LA.

One evening, at dinner, Cox and Hopper got into a political argument. It resulted in Hopper pulling out his Republican Party membership card, Cox snatching it from him and tearing it up.

> "That was very intolerant and rude of me to do that, but I really wanted Dennis to be an icon of the left, but he's not. He's sort of an anarchist but a right wing anarchist. He believes in America. But he is a very fascinating guy and has always been kind to Tod and me. You couldn't have a better boss if you're a writer on a film.'

Backtrack was released in a cut and edited version called *Catchfire* and was attributed to, at Hopper's insistence, the pseudonym favoured by enraged American directors who wish to disown a project: Alan Smithee. Later, Cox and Davies wrote a script about *Che Guevara* for Canal + in France, but it wasn't the romanticised version of events the producers wanted. Since then, they have been working on the script for a film on the life of Luis Buñuel.

After the *Backtrack* job, Cox was then asked to direct another dramatised case history, that of the now legendary Derek Bentley murder case of the early 1950s. He agreed to do it on the condition that it be made in black and white:

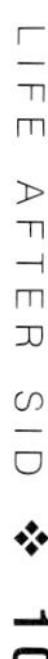

> "I thought the only way the film would work would be if it looked like a movie that was made at that time. As a low budget, 1950s British thriller, it would have been extraordinary. It was somewhat antique and needed to look like a Tony Richardson movie such as *The Loneliness of the Long Distance Runner*."

After scouting for locations, Cox cast the film, which included Christopher Eccelston and Paul Reynolds in the principal roles. The centre piece of the crew was cameraman Gilbert Taylor, the black and white photographer responsible for *A Hard Day's Night* and *Dr Strangelove*. The cast and crew were all ready to go. Cox's agent phoned him: "You haven't been paid. They're refusing to sign your contract because it says the film has to be in black and white and it's been sold as a colour film and the producers haven't told you. They were hoping you would go along with it." Never one to sell out, Cox couldn't go on but says he always knew something was going on:

> "There was a sort of weird, sick feeling to it. If people lie to you, it's part of a continuous process – they don't just lie once, they lie many times. I think it's a shame producers don't have more faith in black and white films. It's the same in Hollywood. The only American directors working today who seem to be able to make films in black and white are Woody Allen, Jim Jarmusch and Spike Lee. But it does seem strange that since rock videos and commercials are made in black and white and their job is to sell products (and they obviously do successfully or they wouldn't be made), why aren't many more films made in black and white now, too? I think it has more to do with the conservative nature of the Hollywood film industry than with audiences. Audiences can take it; Hollywood, it seems, cannot."

Unfortunately for the producers of *Let Him Have It*, not only did they lose their director, they also lost a lot of other people who were involved. Richard Attenborough was to play the hanging judge and Steven Berkoff was going to play the father. They both left, as did Gil Taylor. The picture was later directed by Peter Medak.

Eccleston did not walk. Playing Derek Bentley (the last man in the UK to be hanged for murder) was his big break, having been offered the role out of nowhere:

> "I'd left drama school in 1986 and hadn't worked for three years. If Alex hadn't cast me in the first place,

Medak wouldn't have even seen me. But by that time, for whatever reason, the producers were happy with me as Bentley. Maybe it was because I was cheap!"

Eccleston was disappointed with Medak's film, which turned out more commercial than radical:

> "I think it would have been less Hollywood with Alex and more intelligent. From early discussions it was clear he would have allowed me to get across a more realistic portrayal of Derek as a working class boy. Medak's film was full of compromises. There was no strong stylistic approach. With such challenging subject matter, you need a strong standpoint and trust that the audience will connect with that. Alex was going to show the gang in slow-mo to get across the excitement the kids felt, rather than just making a film that occupied a grey area."

Cox also tried to make a film called *The Battle of Torremolinos*, which had been written by Martin Turner for Lindsay Anderson. Anderson had dropped all current projects after receiving bad reviews for the first time in his career for his film *The Old Crowd*. However, Cox read the script and thought it was very funny. It was the story of the English and Germans re-fighting World War II on the beaches of Spain. Unfortunately, in the mid-Eighties, there was a huge influx of television actors coming into the film industry and directors found themselves having to opt for these rather than stage or film actors:

> "We were stymied because the British film industry was at the time entirely devoted to *The Comic Strip* (as the American industry was beholden to *Saturday Night Live*) and you couldn't get a film on in London without the participation of at least three so-called comics from that dire TV show, or an even worse one called *The Young Ones*. The Spanish thought the script was very funny, but the Germans didn't seem to think it was funny at all. Two years later, the tabloid papers were full of the same phenomenon, the basis of *The Battle of Torremolinos*, which they called Lager Lout-itis."

But by then, it was too late.

Another project on offer for Cox was the sequel to *Robo Cop*. Not surprisingly, he wasn't interested:

> "*Robo Cop 2* wasn't something I would have been good at: too much heroic stuff and things exploding. The cop, whether he's Bruce Willis or Mel Gibson or a robot, is always cracking heads and behaving bestially – but it's supposed to be okay because he's pitted against 'a greater evil'. And I don't find that a particularly interesting set-up for a drama."

Even though Cox wasn't having much success in finding the right sort of directing project, he was still very much in the public eye in Britain. In fact, he was seen by millions of television viewers every week. In 1987, he was asked to take part in a new television series produced by the writer and critic David Thompson for the BBC. The programme was called *The Film Club* and required a different director to introduce two films each week. When it came to the turn of Alex Cox, he was asked to introduce *Point Blank* and *The Long Goodbye*. Usually, the crew would film at the house of the director and have them standing by a mantlepiece. Not having a house in London, Cox persuaded Thompson to shoot his piece at the Lloyds building. His contribution to the series was the only episode to use such an unusual location. This caught the eye of another BBC producer, Nick Jones, and, a year later, Cox was invited back to the BBC and asked to present his own series, called *Moviedrome*.

He agreed and wrote and hosted the introductions to a variety of cult-type films that played each Sunday night on BBC2:

> "Sometimes I worried that people thought I was choosing the films, and there was also the possibility that people would think I had directed them. Admittedly, most were great, including *Sweet Smell of Success*, *Alphaville* and *Dead of Night*. But there were awful ones as well, such as *Diva* and *The Terminator*."

Moviedrome gave Cox the opportunity to talk about international cinema (at a time when the BBC wasn't afraid to show subtitled films), as well as a few 'great American movies' and his favourite genre: the Western. Here are just a few examples…

Les Diaboliques (1954) is a horror film, and yes, it's in French, with subtitles, but please don't be put off! You will not be disappointed. This film is at least 15 times more frightening than *Friday the Twelfth Part Fourteen* or any of the other inane sequels you can rent down at the newsagents. This is a real film, directed by a real film director. And it is really frightening. If you watch *Les Diaboliques* all the way to the end, you will be scared. Guaranteed.

It is very unfortunate, my having to throw myself at your feet like this to try and make you watch this film, but there really does seem to be a lot of resistance to foreign-language films, not only in Britain, but all over Europe. France and Britain are relatively civilised in showing foreign films in their original language, assuming they get shown at all. Germany, Italy and Spain, on the other hand, will generally only screen dubbed foreign movies. And all across the EC the most popular films are American ones, with local products coming a distant second and other nations' movies hardly registering at all.

Imagine a triple bill of Roman Polanski's *Repulsion*, *Les Diaboliques* and Paul Verhoeven's *The Fourth Man*. Three fantastic, sexy, Euro horror films. Pit them against the contemporary Hollywood product – say *Pet Semetary*, *Freddy's Dead* and William Friedkin's *The Guardian*. Why would anybody want to watch films like these, if they could watch films like those?

I can't really tell you what *Les Diaboliques* is about since the plot is fraught with too many strange twists and surprises. Let me instead briefly talk about the director. Henri-Georges Clouzot's second feature, *Le Corbeau*, was made in 1942 and produced by the German-owned Continentale Films. The film's negative and depressing view of provincial French life was seen as German propaganda and as a result Clouzot didn't direct again until 1947 when he made *Quai des Orfevres*, which won the Golden Lion at Venice. Clouzot evolved into a cynical, highly pessimistic film-maker – and also a very brilliant one. His most celebrated film is the adventure drama, *Le Salaire de la Peur* (*Wages of Fear*), which was remade – not badly – by the aforementioned William Friedkin in 1977, before his fall from high estate. *Wages of Fear*, the story of four men paid to truck high explosives through jungles and across mountains in Honduras, is one of the greatest films of all time – it was made entirely in the South of France.

Les Diaboliques has much of the same intensity and mad invention, though it's about women, not men. It features an implacable Simone Signoret and the fabulously beautiful Vera Clouzot, wife of the director. She was also the glamorously cringing love interest in *Wages of Fear*.

Sweet Smell of Success (1957) is the story of a sleazy press agent called Sidney Falco (Tony Curtis), and his life's work currying favour with the sinister and powerful newspaper columnist JJ Hunsecker (Burt Lancaster). Both Curtis and Lancaster are great. Lancaster's character seems to be modelled on the powerful media personality Walter Winchell; he's a friend of senators and big-time Mafiosi. Curtis is always snapping at his heels, barking for scraps. It's a fantastic film, but almost unknown in the US.

It was directed by Alexander Mackendrick who was born in Boston, Massachusetts but educated in Scotland. The director of some of the finest Ealing comedies, including *Whiskey Galore* and *The Ladykillers*, this was his first American film, an incredible indictment of the media and advertising and human relationships and just about everything else. Maybe it was Mackendrick's ex-patriot background that helped him cut through all the bullshit and make a great American film. Other 'foreign directors' who spring to mind are John Schlesinger with *Midnight Cowboy* and Milos Forman with *One Flew Over the Cuckoo's Nest*. Or, flowing the other way, Stanley Kubrick came to Britain and made *Clockwork Orange*, a pretty good movie about us.

Sweet Smell of Success was written by Ernest Lehman and Clifford Odets who did a similar hatchet job on Hollywood with *The Big Knife*. Success was photographed by James Wong Howe, one of the great Hollywood cameramen.

We need heroes and villains, and this film has two of the latter. In the words of Sidney Falco: never forget, "it's in a man's nature to get out there and hustle and get the things he wants."

One from the Heart was the first film Coppola made after *Apocalypse Now*. I think that this was, in a sense, his attempt to come down after creating that enormous epic, which took a lot of energy and several years of production – making instead a small, intimate story about two people and what happens when you try to cheat on your boyfriend or girlfriend.

It is set in Las Vegas, but it was filmed on the sound stages of Coppola's Zoetrope Studios in Hollywood. Zoetrope was a noble attempt to recreate an old-style studio system for the benefit of creative people: in the two years that Coppola owned Zoetrope, before he had to let it go for lack of money, Gene Kelly, Wim Wenders and Jean-Luc Goddard all worked there. Zoetrope may have been a noble endeavour, but it was also the reason why *One from the Heart* doesn't entirely work. There are two things at war in the film. One is the very simple romantic story, and the other is the grandiose element: the $25 million budget, the elaborate sets, the big special-effect dance numbers and the awful songs.

It's not that the songs by Tom Waits and Crystal Gale are bad in themselves; it's only that when you see a man walking upstairs, tripping on an item of a woman's clothing, picking it up, looking at it, frowning and carrying on walking, you don't need to hear a voice on the soundtrack singing: "I'm sick and tired of picking up after you." It's a sort of overkill.

Coppola had to wait a little while longer before he could make a small, cheap film that was really satisfying – that was *Rumblefish*. But *One from the Heart* is interesting. All Coppola's films are interesting. The man can't make a totally useless movie.

Produced, directed and co-written by Billy Wilder in 1951, *Ace in the Hole* (also sometimes called *The Big Carnival*) is the story of a big city reporter (Kirk Douglas) who cynically exploits the plight of a man trapped in a cave on the Navajo reservation in New Mexico.

Today, reporters are generally portrayed in films as well-intentioned, saintly characters, and it's a great pleasure to see one here who's totally self-serving. Of course, he's not alone in this: under Wilder's merciless pen and directorial baton, all the characters get taken to the cleaners. They're all making money or a reputation out of this – including the man who's trapped – because "everybody likes a break".

Wilder is the cinematic equivalent of Vladimir Nabokov. He's completely cynical, without sentimentality, without remorse, and he's as great a craftsman with film as Nabokov was with words. Everything about his films – this one, *Some Like It Hot*, *The Apartment* and, of course, *Sunset Boulevard* – is tuned to perfection. They are films with perfect symmetry.

It's not just that Wilder did everything himself – writing, producing and directing is enough – but he also chose his collaborators with such skill that everywhere you look – at the acting, the editing, the art direction – and everything you hear (listen to the music) appears flawless. This is also the film that teaches you how to strike a match with a typewriter.

In 1968, Dennis Hopper, Peter Fonda, Jack Nicholson, Bob Rafelson and Henry Jaglom made *Easy Rider*, the most successful cult film of all time. It was such a success that it probably isn't a cult film at all, but a mainstream movie. It made a lot of money, and as you know, money signifies quality. Money also conveys power. As a result of making such a successful film, all five guys were given more money to direct more films. Hopper went off to Peru and made *The Last Movie*; Nicholson directed *Drive, He Said*; Henry Jaglom made *A Safe Place*; Bob Rafelson made *Five Easy Pieces*; and Peter Fonda made a western called *The Hired Hand*. Fonda's movie is not a great film. It's one of those acid westerns where the camerawork is all bleary and there are long transitions and the people don't say much. It's not as good as *The Last Movie*; it doesn't have Hopper's madness or breadth of vision. But what's really good about it is that it has a big performance by Warren Oates in the role of Fonda's sidekick, Harris. Warren Oates was a wonderful actor. He was in *Cockfighter*, a film which, because of its accurate depiction of its subject matter, can't be shown in Britain; he was in *Drum, Kid Blue*, *The Shooting*, *Bring Me the Head of Alfredo Garcia*, *Dillinger* and *The Wild Bunch*, among others. If you talk to a really good American actor who's working today – someone like Dennis Hopper, Harry Dean Stanton, Ed Harris – and you ask who they think is the best American actor, living or dead, it is quite likely that they're not going to say Marlon Brando. They'll tell you it's Warren Oates.

Cox was a natural choice to host the BBC series. He was an individual who had himself become somewhat of a cult hero, based on his reputation as a director of films of a genuinely curious and idiosyncratic nature. All of the introductions for each season were filmed over a few days each year. The first season was shot in London, the second in Tucson, the third in Almería. The dark, mysterious backdrops and Cox's eccentricities made this unique series the most interesting forum for weird cult films. *Moviedrome* was very popular and he remained with the programme for seven years. It was also Cox's main source of income. During its run, Cox had moved to Mexico to work on his first film as a director since *Walker*.

Chapter Six

Escape

You can't escape from what you're trying to escape from,
and the lesson of the road is that there is no lesson of the road.
Rudy Wurlitzer

No man has ever prospered or died happily outside the law.
GD Hadfield, US Marine Commander in Nicaragua to AC Sandino, 12 July 1927

In the winter of 1986, Cox had been scouting locations for *Walker* in Northern Mexico with producer Lorenzo O'Brien. They hadn't planned to shoot in Mexico but had to go there to allay the fears of the producers, who were already afraid of shooting in war-torn Nicaragua. In the event, *Walker* was made in Nicaragua but the trip to Mexico hadn't been a wasted one.

On the mountain road between Durango and Mazatlan, Cox and O'Brien found themselves caught in a giant traffic jam. A lorry had jack-knifed at the foot of Devil's Backbone Mountain. Marooned in their van, they were regaled with stories by their driver, a former member of the Federal Highway Patrol. He told them a number of fascinating tales of what it was like to be a highway cop in Mexico.

Captivated by the driver's stories, O'Brien began work on a screenplay *Federal de Caminos* and, in 1990, returned to Mexico, with Cox, in search of the driver. They found him in Mexico City and he agreed to let them tape-record the history of his career in the Federal Highway Patrol as well as his domestic life in which he was negotiating two families that he had running in two towns simultaneously. Recalling the conversations he had with the driver for an interview on the official Alex Cox internet website [www.alexcox.com], Cox says that, interestingly, one story that he remembers the most never actually made it into the film.

"He had stopped a car at night on a long highway called the Recta de Matehuala. A gringo was at the wheel. The guy had the stereo cranked way up, and it was playing 'Sympathy for the Devil'. Our young cop knew the gringo was stoned and he could probably bust him, but he thought, what the heck? It might turn out to be a hassle, maybe the gringo had lawyers and money, and it was late at night. He turned his back on the guy for just a moment, planning to let him go, and he heard this little click-click sound...

"Our friend recognised the lock-and-load of an Uzi. He threw himself to the ground just as the shooting began, scrambled off into the dirt and dark, into the nopal-filled night, and lay there, in a cactus patch, with a bullet in his leg, pretending to be dead and listening as the Camaro started up and drove away, hearing the Rolling Stones grow fainter and finally disappear. And of course, his car had been destroyed in the firefight and he had to walk back, with a bullet in his leg, to the destacamento.

"I loved that story when I first heard it, because it seemed to be about how no good deed goes unpunished, and the impossibility of ever behaving properly or achieving anything. 'God helps the bad when they outnumber the good,' the Mexicans say, and they are absolutely right. And yet it is essential that we do the right thing, as we can, that we not behave as badly as the monsters that confront us, that we have our own code, and do our best to live by it...

"Mexico is a great teacher of this lesson. Because, no matter how the Mexicans are abused by their powerful neighbour to the north, no matter how much their politicians are bribed and their cops corrupted, they always retain a high degree of dignity and repose, a sense of politeness and personal honour and correctness that can never, ever, be defeated. The poorest man in Zacatecas or Durango or Cuahuila will address a stranger with such courtesy, such absolute formal respect, and will hope to be dealt with courteously in return. 'Bievenidos, senor, caballero. You have taken possession of your house.' 'Now I must take my leave of you.' 'Here you always have your home.' 'Hopefully we will see each other again before too long'. 'Indeed so – if God wills it.'

"Alfonso Arau, the director of *Like Water for Chocolate*, told me he didn't like *Highway Patrolman* because the world it depicted was ugly. Well, perhaps it is. In that case, I am doubly lucky. Because the Mexicans have let me paint a sometimes dark picture of the world in which they live – and that is a testament to their tolerance and sophistication."

After meeting with the driver again, later in 1991, O'Brien's screenplay attracted the attention of Marubeni, a Japanese trading company interested in financing films. Cox's *Straight to Hell* had just had a smash opening in Japan and the company put up a modest budget of $1.5 million for Cox to make *Highway Patrolman* (*El Patrullero*). The fact that O'Brien's script was in Spanish didn't faze them because the film would be subtitled in Japanese.

With work due to begin on *Highway Patrolman* in late April 1991, Cox began to educate himself before directing his first Mexican feature. He had already seen Buñuel's Mexican films (*Los Olvidados*, *El*, *Exterminating Angel*) and the Mexican-based features of Huston and Peckinpah. But these were all films by foreigners. Cox decided to try to see a wider selection of old and recent Mexican films. In November 1995, Cox wrote a lengthy article in praise of Mexican cinema for *Film Comment* magazine entitled *Roads to the South*. Although a lot has changed in regard to the Mexican film industry since then, Cox's commentary on the variety of Mexican films and the history of how such pictures were funded remain relevant and compelling. The article is reproduced here…

For a country with a long and distinguished cinema history, the task I had set myself was not easy. Though certain Mexican classics such as *Vamonos con Pancho Villa!* (1936) have been preserved and are regularly screened by the underfunded government film institute Cineteca, many have disappeared. A fire in the Eighties destroyed countless original positives and negatives. Moreover, Televisa, the gigantic private televisual conglomerate, owns the rights to many features it never screens. The great period of Mexican cinema – the Forties and Fifties, when Buñuel and Emilio 'El Indio' Fernandez produced some of their best work – is almost invisible today. Try as they might, our Mexico City production office could not find a copy of Fernandez's classic *La Perla* (after Steinbeck) on tape or film. Most of his other films were likewise unavailable.

Eventually I secured a copy of *Rio Escondido* (1947) – widely distributed internationally as *Hidden River* and generally regarded as one of the director's lesser efforts – and made a happy discovery: this story of a fanatical young schoolteacher in an impoverished rural community is an extraordinary film, both visually and from a narrative point of view. Previously I had known Fernandez only as a portrayer of heavies for Peckinpah and Huston. Here El Indio – the legendary macho who once shot a film critic – delivers a powerful feminist tale. The heroine, though prone to fits of melancholy, is indomitable. Against all odds, she teaches a class of destitute kids to read; she faces down and humiliates a malevolent young hidalgo; when the landowner gets drunk and tries to rape her, she shoots him dead. Given the quiveringly omnipresent sexism of so many modern films, it was a real charge to see *Rio Escondido*. I inquired at the office if it was an exception, or if Fernandez put strong women characters in all his films. "Oh yes," was the reply, "they're all like that."

The camerawork by Gabriel Figueroa, one of the world's greatest black-and-white cinematographers, is typically impressive. His compositions are stark, expressionist: white-walled buildings, cacti, dusty streets leading to broad, empty plazas in which people gather, posed like desert rock formations under a sunset sky gilled with spectacular clouds. His camera movement often demonstrates a sophisticated simplicity, as when he opens on a medium shot of the heroine, moves slightly to incorporate the villain in a two-shot, and ends in a single on him as Maria Felix slips from the frame (a shot which Miguel Garzon and I copied in *Highway Patrolman* in the scene where Roberto Sosa realises his superiors are on to his racket). Fernandez and Figueroa's 1949 *Pueblerina* (sometimes on Spanish-speaking TV) is just as strong: massively emotional, tragic, photographed like a series of Ansel Adams plates.

Spanish cinema of the same period had to contend with the Franco regime's censorship. In Mexico the ruling Institutional Revolutionary Party (PRI), though repressive in many ways, has viewed culture as a source of national unity and pride. Hence the establishment of the Cineteca and various schemes to promote feature film production, including a now-defunct National Film Bank. The most recent was the establishment, in 1983, of a government-sponsored office, IMCINE, to finance and to promote Mexican film. The single largest producer of Mexican films and the most influential, IMCINE is an umbrella organisation that produces, exhibits and originally distributed the majority of Mexico's films, as well as owning a dozen movie theatres and the Churubusco–Azteca studios, built in the Forties by RKO and several private investors. Since IMCINE's inception, the government has privatised more and more of it, most notably in the divestment of COTSA, its distribution arm, in the early Nineties. Many of the COTSA theatres were picked up by US exhibitors which tend to show American films at exorbitant prices.

IMCINE provokes both fury and loyalty from Mexican film-makers. As a domestic producer and promoter of selected Mexican films abroad, with the power to provide or deny funding to film-makers, it could hardly avoid being called political. Its future under the Zedillo presidency is uncertain, yet one only has to remember the fierceness of the Americans' attack on European film subsidies under GATT, and the determination with which the French opposed it, to realise something significant is at stake here. In 1994 the US threatened to sue the Canadian Government under the

▲ Blanca Guerra and Alex Cox in Arturo Ripstein's *La Reina de la Nocha*.

terms of NAFTA, insisting that Canadian support of film-makers was an unfair trading practice. If state support for cinema continues in Mexico, the Zedillo regime may also face a legal challenge from the US.

Whether or not IMCINE survives, popular cinema is still alive and well in Mexico – mainly as sex comedies and cop dramas like *AR-15* and *La Muerte de un Federal de Caminos*. But Hollywood movies increasingly dominate the market and, with rare exceptions, Mexican 'art' films are seldom screened.

The principal exponent of Mexican art cinema for the last 30 years – and a beneficiary of IMCINE's fiscal support – is Arturo Ripstein Jr. His first film was a violent, spaghetti-ish Western, *Tiempo de Morir* (1965), produced by his father, Arturo Sr. It was an unfortunate collaboration, and father and son did not work together again for almost three decades. (Family bonds became a crucial element of Ripstein's subsequent films.) Ripstein had been Buñuel's assistant director on *El Angel Exterminador*, and if there is any film-maker in the world who can be said to have inherited Buñuel's mantle, Ripstein is a prime candidate. Though not a visual surrealist, he shares many of the master's preoccupations, in particular, the incestuous horrors of domesticity. At times, his films resemble particularly unsettling soap operas: Ripstein – who actually has directed soaps for Televisa as a survival tactic – concentrates nowadays entirely on painful intimacies in long take, without the respite of close-ups or cutaways.

El Castillo de la Pureza (*The Castle of Purity*, 1973) is Ripstein's tale – based on a news item – of a fanatical bourgeois who never lets his family leave the house; he goes to work each day, leaving them locked indoors, to protect them from the contamination of the outside world. Disaster, predictably, ensues. *Lugar Sin Limites* (*The Place Without Limits*, 1977) is the story of a flamboyant gay man and his platonic love affair with the madame of a small-town brothel; he is eventually murdered by machos unsure of their own gender orientation. The hero is played by Roberto Cobo, whom Buñuel had cast as the baddest of the street urchins in *Los Olvidados* a quarter-century before. Shot in bright colours by Miguel Garzon, rural environment as El Indio's films – though the sexual angle is far more convoluted.

In 1994 Ripstein's *La Reina de la Noche* (*Queen of the Night*) was Mexico's entry at Cannes (the first time in 20 years a Mexican film had been accepted in the main competition; on the previous occasion the director was also Ripstein). The story of a tragic cabaret singer (sometimes it seems that almost all Mexican movies are set in cabarets or at least feature cabaret sequences), *La Reina de la Noche* was written by Ripstein's long-time screenwriter and partner Paz Alicia Garciadiego, and stars some of Mexico's best actors – Patricia Reyes Spindola, Blanca Guerra, Alberto Estrella, Roberto Sosa and Ana Ofelia Murguia, outstanding as the characteristically Ripsteinian monstrous mother. (I cannot judge *La Reina de la Noche* dispassionately since I am in it: the director was mad enough to cast me in a supporting role.) Ripstein is not for all tastes. His films deal in cruelty, irony, tragedy. They depict seriously disturbed characters with the most malevolent or pathetic motives. His austere long takes are intricately planned beforehand; he is meticulous about composition. His more recent films are long (*Principio y Fin/The Beginning and the End* runs over three hours), and, given their themes of incest, child abuse, mental cruelty, murder and abortion, are often harrowing. The last reel of *Principio y Fin* is a single take, nine and a half minutes long, featuring a double suicide by sister and brother. The camera follows the action from street level, upstairs, downstairs, through a sauna and a set of steam room cubicles, and out on to a roof. For my money, Ripstein is one of the best and most interesting directors working today.

Talents such as Ripstein and Jorge Fons were at the forefront of the Seventies renaissance in Mexican art cinema; in the Sixties, when Mexican film was at its lowest ebb, they were obliged to work on genre subjects (Ripstein scripted *Cinco mil Dollares de Recompensa/Five Thousand Dollars Reward*, 1972, for Fons). Of the bizarre series of what Ripstein calls 'Chilli-Westerns,' the most notable exponent was the director Alberto Mariscal, who brought them some of the same weird atmosphere that David Lynch unleashed on *Leave it to Beaverland*.

Working on sets built for US Westerns like the Henry Hathaway–John Wayne *The Sons of Katie Elder*, Mariscal made *Todo por Nada* (*All for Nothing*, 1968), which as its title suggests has little to commend it, and *El Tunco Maclovio* (1969) – one of the looniest Westerns ever made. *El Tunco*, shot partially in a Zacatecas cactus forest and graced with a musical score dominated by guitar white noise, is the story of a one-armed bounty hunter in an obsessive revenge partnership with a little kid. At one point the hero believes he has killed his partner and falls to his knees, wailing and hitting himself with his pistol. After a couple of minutes of this, the kid comes back to life and they resume the adventure.

Los Marcados (*The Branded*, 1972) is even more baroque and madder, in a variety of ways. It features massacres, an old Chinese tattoo artist and a gang of homosexual outlaws who act scenes from Shakespeare. Ignored by English-speaking critics, these films are among the very few Mexican features to have gained a wide release in English-language versions. (*Los Marcados* was a provincial action-picture hit in Britain in the early Seventies.) Today Mariscal's Westerns are as hard to find in the US as *La Perla* is in Mexico – but you might try the Hispanic section at the videostore.

Another original talent who surfaced at this time was Paul Leduc. A Mexican despite his francophronic name, his speciality has been films without dialogue. He made his reputation with Reed: *Insurgent Mexico* (1971) and later scored with a biography of Frida Kahlo, *Frida* (1984), which consists of an appealing series of tableaux from her life (the actors Ofelia Medina and Juan Gurrolla as Diego Rivera bearing a strong resemblance to their characters). Leduc is the most consistently political of modern Mexican directors and has made several co-productions with IMCINE and the Cuban National Film Institute, ICAIC. His most recent works are *Latino Bar* (1991) and *Dollar Mambo* (1993), the latter recreating the US invasion of Panama within the confines of a rundown waterfront cabaret. (I am not making it up – all these films really do take place in cabarets!) Though Leduc's experiments without dialogue are not always successful, at least he is experimenting, and there is much to enjoy and to appreciate in his pictures. The arrival of the US Marines in *Dollar Mambo* – alien toys dropping from a miniature helicopter – sticks in the mind, a Caribbean riposte to *ET*.

By the Eighties, Mexican cinema had reached a crossroads. Here was a country with a film-making tradition as old as that of the US, possessed of technicians and actors to equal any in the world. American producers were flocking south to make Mexican-based mega-productions like *Total Recall*, *Fat Man and Little Boy* (whose producers rebuilt Los Alamos in Durango), *Licence to Kill* and *Medicine Man*. Would Mexico go the way of the UK, abandoning all but the most minor of domestic film production so as to serve the American production line of Spielberg, Lucas and James Bond? Or would the dual domestic industries – popular and art – survive? The deal had, of course, gone badly for Britain, as a rising pound caused Americans to abandon Blighty, with no resurgence of domestic feature production to take their place. In

Mexico, IMF-mandated 'reforms' and a stronger peso started working the same way, translating into higher prices and encouraging American producers to look further south, to Chile, Argentina and Peru. But Mexican domestic production held its ground more or less. If anything, while the popular sector diminished (mainly due to TV), the art sector increased, even venturing into uncharted waters: in secret, far from IMCINE and the studios, director Jorge Fons began in 1989 to make a film that explored one of the darkest moments of Mexico's recent past.

'68 is still remembered as a year of civil disturbance and unrest. The Tlatelolco Massacre of that year was largely ignored by the outside world, but within Mexico it has never been forgotten. On the evening of October 1, several thousand students had gathered for a peaceful demonstration near the Plaza of Three Cultures in a residential barrio. Their grievances were generic of the time, highlighted by what they saw as the government's gratuitous waste of public money on the Olympic Games. The Army and Judicial Police ringed the open plaza and as it grew dark, a helicopter dropped flares into the crowd. Then the police and troops opened fire. No one knows how many students and passers-by died that night. The wounded and the dead were trucked away, never to be seen again, while subsidiary massacres broke out all over town. The international press, present in large numbers for the official opening of the Games, effectively abetted a cover-up of the massacre, or if they did file, their stories were unprinted and unbroadcast by the media that didn't want to spoil the show. Current 'official' estimates admit 200–250 students slain; unofficial estimates – those of the families of the missing – suggest at least 2–3000 died. (When we were shooting *Death and the Compass* in the Convent of San Ildefonso, now part of the Autonomous University of Mexico, several crew members took me to see the bullet holes around the front door of this small University annex.)

In April 1991, five days before I left for Mexico to begin shooting *Highway Patrolman*, Nick Jones, producer of *Moviedrome*, and I watched *Rojo Amanecer* (Red Sunrise), the film Fons made about the massacre. Banned for two years, the film is now a sensation in Mexico. We watched it twice. It is one of the best movies I've ever seen. *Rojo Amanecer* is a milestone – not only in Mexican cinema but in film history. The story unfolds entirely within the confines of a lower-middle-class apartment overlooking Tlatelolco. The mother (Maria Rojo) is an ama de casa, raising three children in a two-bedroom flat. The father (actor–producer Hector Bonilla) is a government bureaucrat. Their older children (played by the brothers Bruno and Damien Bichir) plan to attend the demonstration; the youngest kids prefer to play with friends or stay home.

In *Rojo Amanecer* the camera never looks into the plaza; we never see the massacre itself, only its effect on the inhabitants of the tiny flat. After the first wave of killing, troops and plainclothes police scour the apartment buildings looking for survivors. Simultaneously, several students, some of them wounded, take refuge in the apartment. By dawn, three generations of Mexicans – reactionary grandfather (a scene-stealing performance by the late Jorge Fegan), conservative parents, radical and innocent children – are all dead. Only a 4-year-old remains, descending the endless staircases of the giant flatblock to join the ranks of homeless children – Buñuel's 'forgotten ones' – on the streets below.

The film was made, needless to say, without governmental finance, on a stage set in a warehouse. The building, belonging to Mexico City's Moviecam dealer, was not soundproofed, which accounts for a certain unnatural perspective on the dialogue tracks. Production took place in strictest secrecy on a tight schedule. Last-minute alterations became necessary when the set, built to the exact dimensions of a Tlatelolco flat, didn't allow cinematographer Miguel Garzon room to manoeuvre. When the film was finished, it was immediately banned – supposedly not on the orders of President Salinas, but on those of the even more powerful Presidential Military Guard. *Rojo Amanecer* was not the first film to be banned by the State. Up until this time, all feature scripts had to be submitted to the government-run Cinematografia for approval, and State censors had been an omnipresent feature on the sets of foreign-financed films. But times had changed. There was a great desire on the part of many people to confront the suppressed reality of their history; and film-makers and intellectuals (some of whom had seen the film on video) rallied to Fons's support. When the Salinas government caved in to popular demand and allowed the public screening of *Rojo Amanecer*, the nature of film production in Mexico was forever changed. Had the film not been popular, things might have gone on as before, but *Rojo Amanecer* was a runaway success – both at the cinema and on video, one of the biggest-grossing domestic features of all time. I've seen it several times and never fail to be astonished by its intensity and its honesty. Fons's direction is outstanding. Garzon's camerawork so at the service of the story that it never once draws attention to itself and the performances are particularly strong.

But success at home was no guarantee of recognition abroad. Despite winning a special prize at San Sebastian (where reportedly Ken Loach threatened to resign from the jury unless the film was honoured in some way), *Rojo Amanecer* has received little or no support outside Mexico. IMCINE had not produced the film and chose to ignore it, while co-producer Valentin Trujillo did little to promote it overseas. The Havana Film Festival, seeking increased ties with IMCINE and the Mexican government, refused to screen it (two years later they gave Best Film and Best Actor awards to an insipid Mexican production, Jaime Humberto Hermosilla's *La Tarea*). American and European distributors, knowing nothing of the Tlatelolco Massacre and caring less, did not pick up the film, although it did play at certain US festivals.

Did *Rojo Amanecer* prove to be the watershed for a new, political Mexican cinema? Not entirely. Though they are clearly aware of politics. Ripstein and Fons share concerns that are primarily familial and social – as were those of Don Luis Buñuel. *Rojo Amanecer* was turned into a successful stage play, and Fons has worked in television since: his feature, *El Callejon de Milagros* (*Miracle Alley*) premiered in Berlin in 1995. The generation that follows Fons and Ripstein seems more comfortable with genre homages than with overt politics.

But there was no going back, and Mexican film-makers have since found themselves possessed of a new freedom of choice in the subjects they can portray. Since the domestic success of *Rojo Amanecer*, Mexican art cinema has fallen into two categories: films that tend to be more personal and more ambiguously political, such as *Pueblo de Madera (Timber Town)*, *La Vida Conjugal (Married Life)*, *Angel de Fuego (Angel of Fire)*, *Lolo* and *Cabeza de Vaca*; and films strategically gauged to please an international or American audience – *Solo con tu Pareja (Love in the Time of Hysteria)*, *La Invention de Cronos (Cronos)* and the hyper-successful *Como Agua para Chocolate (Like Water for Chocolate)*.

Como Agua para Chocolate (1992), directed by Alfonso Arau and based on the novel by his then-wife Laura Esquivel, is the film most readers of this book will have seen. So successful has Arau's film been, both in Mexico and internationally, that I hope I will be forgiven for not giving it more space and attention here. It follows the grand Mexican tradition of films of rural life, but from the point of view of apparent aristocrats. It is interesting to compare it to *Pueblo de Madera* and *La Mujer de Benjamin*, made a couple of years earlier. *Pueblo* (1991) is an ensemble story of life in an impoverished lumber town in the state of Durango; for the most part it is resolutely naturalistic and unspectacular. *La Mujer de Benjamin* (1991), directed by Carlos Carrera, is the ironic tale of a small-town half-wit (brilliantly underplayed by Eduardo Lopez Rojas) who kidnaps the local girl of his dreams. Both films have a hard edge to them, and a real sense of humour, whereas *Como Agua para Chocolate* seems to me romanticised to the point of stickiness. The shots are all soft-focus; there are so many heaving breasts, so many pregnant sighs, that one might mistake it for the movie version of a Barbara Cartland novel.

Pueblo de Madera and *La Mujer de Benjamin* barely come close to having sentimental moments: they seem very real in their depiction of provincial life. But *Como Agua para Chocolate* is no more about Mexico than *The Lion King* is about Africa: both are syrupy fantasies and highly popular as a result. Director, cast, cinematographers and crew deserve all praise for their ability to reproduce the Merchant–Ivory/Masterpiece Theatre look on an incredibly tiny budget; the film is a tribute to their technical excellence and ingenuity.

Solo con tu Pareja (1991), an urban comedy about a Mexico City playboy who thinks he has AIDS, shot in MTV style by Alfonso Cuaron, earned its director an invitation to Hollywood (where he then directed *A Little Princess*). *La Invention de Cronos* (1992), a film with good special effects but questionable acting, did likewise for its director, SFX make-up maestro Guillermo del Toro. Michael Donnelly, the American producer of Ripstein's *Mujer del Puerto*, observes that *Cronos* succeeds not only as an internationally viable horror picture but as part of a Mexican film tradition – the horror pictures of the Thirties and the horror/exploitation genre of the Sixties, films with evocative titles like *El Santo* and the *Guanajuato Mummy!*

The transit of Arau, Cuaron and del Toro to Los Angeles replicates an exodus occurring all over the Third World, from London to Lima, as talented directors (especially first-timers) are imported by the studios to develop American-style feature films. Peru's leading 'art' director, Francisco Lombardi, remains in Lima financing his own features – in 1994, a version of Dostoyevsky's *Crime and Punishment* entitled *Sin Sompasion* – from the revenues of his own soccer team. His compatriot Luis Llosa, formerly a maker of 'quickies' for Roger Corman, now directs big-budget action vehicles like *Sniper* and *The Specialist* in the States.

Will this schism continue? Probably. The more commercially minded Mexican directors will inevitably gravitate northward, while their more picante colleagues will remain on native soil. Yet cross-cultural pollination will continue: Leduc expands his Central and South American contacts; Werner Herzog promises to bring Mexico to Zoetrope-backed *Conquest of the Americas*; and there is much interest in the director Dana Rothberg (*Angel de Fuego*).

Angel de Fuego (1991) is the story of a fire-eater, played by Evangelina Sosa. It was critically compared to Jodorowsky's films (presumably because it is set in a circus) but in fact has more in common with the work of Ripstein – especially with *La Mujer del Puerto*, in which Sosa also starred. The most noted feature of *Angel* was the casting of Evangelina and Roberto Sosa, real-life sister and brother, as obsessed lovers; both are excellent.

The younger generation of film-makers continues to produce strange and surprising offerings. Francisco Athies's *Lolo* (1993) is a tremendous mixture of soap-operatic high drama, cartoon-like urban nightmare and real tragedy. It features an outstanding performance by Damian Alcazar as a sympathetic, corrupt cop and sterling work by Roberto Sosa as the hapless hero, caught in a web of stupid but inexorable events. *Lolo*'s message is that mundane doings can have horrific results: it would make a great double bill with *Sin Compasion*. Some striking images – the cinematographer was Jorge Medina – suggest conscious allusions to Figueroa, Fernandez and Buñuel.

Carlos Carrera's second feature, *La Vida Conjugal* (1993), surpasses his highly entertaining *Mujer de Benjamin* in speed, complexity and romantic cynicism: it is a black comedy that unfolds over 60 years as a Guadalajaran couple, brilliantly played by Socorro Bonilla and Alonso Echanove, do all in their power to destroy each other, remaining all the while in love. Carrera began as an animator. His first two films show he has the potential to follow Ripstein and Arau out into the international market. It is great to see a new talent such as his emerging from Mexico at a particularly uncertain time.

The Zedillo presidency will continue to support the cinematic arts. But nothing is certain, and there is talk of state money for co-productions, rather than for purely domestic films. (In March 1995 IMCINE announced that owing to economic conditions it would support only five films per year, down from 10–15 per year before that.) On a general level, one hopes that public money will be found for a unique

from the director of "REPO MAN" and "SID & NANCY"
(Winner) Best Actor
–San Sebastian Film Festival
"Vibrantly alive...by far Cox's best film since his wry surreal comedy 'Repo Man.'"
–Kevin Thomas/L.A. TIMES
AN ALEX COX FILM
HIGHWAY
PATROLMAN
In Association With CABLE HOGUE CO. LTD. Presents A TOGETHER BROTHERS/ULTRA FILMS Production Of An ALEX COX FILM
Starring ROBERTO SOSA BRUNO BICHIR VANESSA BAUCHE ZAIDE SILVIA GUTIERREZ PEDRO ARMENDARIZ, JR.
GOMEZ CRUZ EDUARDO LOPEZ ROJAS Executive Producer KUNIAKI NEGISHI Co-Producer JEAN-MICHEL LACOR
SANDOVAL/CLAUDIA BECKER Music by ZANDER SCHLOSS Edited by CARLOS PUENTE Production Designer CECILIA MONTIEL
RECORDED IN ULTRA·STEREO
Director of Photography MIGUEL GARZON Written and Produced by LORENZO O'BRIEN Directed by ALEX COX
FIRST LOOK PICTURES RELEASING

▲ Zaide Silvia Gutierrez as Griselda with Roberto Sosa as Pedro.

cultural asset. On a personal level, I hope that Mexico will remain as generous and receptive to foreign film-makers as she has been to me. The crews of my Mexican films were the best I ever worked with and I feel the deepest gratitude and warmth toward my Mexican collaborators, especially casting director Claudia Becker, assistant directors Miguel Lima and Rene Villareal, actors Pedro Armendariz Jr and Roberto Sosa, and my editor and compa Carlos Puente Ortega.

'Personal' film-makers nowadays must either be very rich or very rootless. Being of the latter kind, I hope my criticisms will be taken in a spirit of respect and amistad. For me, Mexico has always felt like home.

Having acquainted himself with a whole range of Mexican features and now feeling conversant with the Mexican way, in April 1991, Cox set off south with Lorenzo O'Brien and production designer Cecilia Montiel. O'Brien and Montiel are both

▲ Roberto Sosa as Pedro at the Training Academy.

Peruvian. Cox has pointed out that since he is British, they were the only 'aliens' involved in the film because, apart from them, he used a completely Mexican crew. With the $1.5 million dollar budget, *Highway Patrolman* was, at the time the most expensive native Mexican film. Obviously with the senseless Schwarzenegger action/sci-fi pic *Total Recall* having been made there a year earlier, Mexico had been home to much more expensive films, but as far as Mexican nationality films were concerned *Highway Patrolman* was a big film.

An intense character study of Pedro Rojas (Roberto Sosa), initially, we see him at the police training academy, where the sergeant informs the class of the first law of procedure: "they're always guilty of something; you pull them over first and figure out what it is later." During training, cadets have to wash the chief's car and mow his lawn. But the film is more about domestic life than life in the police force.

Pedro's mother and siblings support him in his new career, but his father doesn't want to know and fails to turn up for his graduation ceremony. Having been assigned 'the pig route' for not meeting the ticket quota, he meets Griselda (Zaide Silvia Gutierrez), a farm-owner he allows to escape without a ticket, the woman who soon becomes his wife. Feeling more sympathy with the criminals than with the laws he has to enforce, Pedro begins taking bribes. From this point, the film is one of small disasters. After getting involved with a young drug-addicted prostitute, Maribel

(Vanessa Bauche), he finds himself under increasing pressure to support both her and his wife. He takes more and more bribes, steals from accident victims and hatches a plan to get the better of the drug dealers.

Various incidents build up and slowly crush him. He is shot in the leg and will be crippled for life; he smashes up one of the force's newest patrol cars and is assigned to the unit's oldest wreck of a vehicle; after a drunken night with Maribel, his wife nearly kills him in a terrifying knife attack; his father dies and his best friend is killed. In the end, the viewer feels great sympathy for this Everyman figure, a character Cox has neither sentimentalised nor treated like a villain. He is one of us, a human being with a moral centre. Again, it doesn't matter that this is a Mexican feature. Forget geography. Unlike the out-of-this-world punker Otto and the crazed misplaced extremism of Sid, Pedro is an everyday guy, taking the world on his shoulders in the way we have to, and is therefore far more believable than any Hollywood cop. Despite Cox being an admirer of road movies such as Monte Hellman's *Two-Lane Blacktop*, his film is less about being on the road and more an anti-action movie. Besides, with a scene where the ghost of Pedro's father turns up, it would have been impossible for Cox to make a traditional American police movie.

Pedro finally sets a trap for Maribel's cocaine supplier Emilio. In a shoot-out, Pedro kills him. Unexpectedly, he quits the force to manage his wife's farm and continues to

▼ Everyman Pedro on duty.

support the junkie prostitute girlfriend at the same time, with the threat hanging over him that she could quite easily return to the brothel. He remains trapped in the system. What else can he do? This is reality. The film's whole ethos is captured in the final shot in which a sign on the side of the road reads, 'Paying Taxes is Participating', a trap that Pedro got caught in by always paying some sort of tax. Who better to warn us of the consequences of participating in the system than Alex Cox?

Highway Patrolman was filmed with a hand-held camera using virtuoso long single takes. There are only 187 cuts in the entire film. These uninterrupted sequences allow the action to unfold in the frame itself rather than movements created by editing. The audience can discover the heart of the material rather than allowing the camera to discover it for them.

Cox adopted this approach because he had become sick of the formulaic editing style of the modern American or British film:

> "You can completely predict when the cuts are coming, whether it's a $10 000 movie made in the American South West by teenagers or whether it's a Martin Scorsese film. Critics will go crazy about a film like *Goodfellas* and draw your attention to a *plano secuencia*, a single camera move down some stairs and through a restaurant kitchen. But that's only one shot! The bulk of Scorsese's films is mundane inter-cutting of close-ups and it is a terribly depressing and enervating style of film-making that takes away all energy and surprise."

Cox had already experimented with the long-take sequences with a *plano secuencia* in *Walker*, but had been unable to expand on this after being blacklisted by studios following that film's release. As a result of the difficulty of finding money to make films in the years that followed, Cox had a lot of time to really think about innovative film-making. He realised he should try to make films that avoided internal editing and inter-cutting of close-ups. He wanted to follow a style that was more 'organic' and more like the theatre, only editing if there was a change of time, a change of location or a change of point of view. These were the rules he followed for *Highway Patrolman* and for all of his recent films:

> "...it's amazing what a director can do when he is freed from the traditional limitations imposed on one by Hollywood films. We cast and shot *Highway Patrolman* exactly as I envisioned it. It is the most naturalistic film I've ever made. The most organic. I didn't feel forced or obligated to concede creative elements to pre-conceived notions about what films must be."

DIARY OF ALEX COX – THE MAKING OF *HIGHWAY PATROLMAN*

1991

18 April Lorenzo meets with Mexican Federal Highway Patrol officials, who want to know if he is homosexual or hates his father. They refuse to give us assistance; Lorenzo agrees to change the title of the script; Cecilia has to create a new, fictitious highway police force with distinctive badges, logos, uniforms and cars – the 'Patrulla Nacional de Carreteras' or PNDC. The same day I meet Miguel Garzon, the cinematographer of *Rojo Amanecer*. We sign him up.

3 June *El Patrullero* (as our film is now known) begins shooting in the northern town of Parras, Coahuila. Playing the role of the *Highway Patrolman* is a brilliant young actor, Roberto Sosa – 21 years old, he has already appeared in 30 films. He is one of the best actors I have worked with, perhaps the best. (That night we attend a 'lucha libre' wrestling match and wander the streets of Parras – they look strangely familiar. It turns out that this is where Sam Peckinpah shot the bank robbery in *The Wild Bunch*! None of us knew this till tonight.)

5 June On the road from Parras to Gomez Palacio, we shoot the scene where Pedro is visited by the ghost of his father (Eduardo Lopez Rojas). After weeks of brilliant sunshine, a windstorm and a bank of dark clouds arrive, right on cue for the spectral scene.

8 June At the Ojuela Mines we film the scene where Pedro crosses the suspension bridge. How wonderful that Sosa is not afraid of playing scared! Shadows drift overhead and once again we're blessed with perfect light – the shot looks like a Jose Velasco landscape.

14 June We film at an isolated railway station with Jorge Russek, the scene where Pedro takes his first bribe. Russek is another generation of actor entirely – he worked for Huston, Peckinpah and 'El Indio' Fernandez – but his and Sosa's styles complement each other. We are shooting everything in single takes – today's shot is Miguel Garzon's most difficult one yet, and he pulls it off on Take 6, with aplomb.

▲ On location in Mexico for *Highway Patrolman*.

17–22 June A week in and around Durango. We shoot the rural cop shop, the scenes where Pedro arrests the governor's son and takes toys to the orphanage. (The nun is played by our casting director, Claudia Becker.) Three weeks in, we are running dead on schedule – the long takes make shooting more difficult, but more efficient.

24 June In Sombrerete, Zacatecas, Miguel shoots another exceedingly difficult shot – the death of Pedro's best friend, Anibal (Bruno Bichir). Afterwards, Roberto and I draw maps on our scripts and marvel at how a crew of 60 managed to conceal themselves behind plants, rocks, the camera, so that Pedro and Anibal seem entirely alone.

1 July Farewell to the hot springs of Durango and Zacatecas. We return to Mexico City to shoot the Police Academy and diverse interiors – our first is a hand-held crane shot inside a downtown cabaret (as we've mentioned, all Mexican films must include a cabaret scene). Garzon and Montiel continue to astonish: they are the best 'eyes' I have ever had.

▲ Alex Cox chatting with Roberto Sosa.

❮❮ Roberto Sosa (right) with Bruno Bichir discussing the benefits of air-cooled engines.

▲ Down a tough road – another disaster in the life of a highway patrolman.

11 July — We shoot the scene where Pedro graduates from the Academy. At 1325 a total eclipse occurs as we are filming. The strangest light conditions, dark above with blue horizons insufficient to register on film! Champagne.

16 July — The last evening of our six and a half week shoot – also Garzon's longest hand-held shot, following the inebriated Pedro through his house, pursued by his knife-wielding wife Griselda (Zaide Silvia Guttierez – my favourite Mexican actress). Four takes and the seven-minute scene is in the can. Leaving the set, Lorenzo, Cecilia and I are doused with blue paint – our official 'baptism' by the technicians of the STIC the Mexican film union, whose ranks we have just been allowed to join!

30 Oct — We sat down with Kuniaki Negishi, our Executive Producer, to watch the first answer print of *Highway Patrolman*. Negi-san declared himself well-pleased with his 'Samurai Film'.

Highway Patrolman debuted at the San Sebastian Film Festival in 1992, where Roberto

▲ "One of the best actors I have worked with, perhaps the best." Cox on Sosa.

Sosa received the Best Actor Award for his performance as Pedro. Having just completed the film at the end of 1991, Cox was immediately offered another job. He was contacted by the BBC in London who had been approached by a Spanish producer involved in organising various productions to celebrate the 500th anniversary of the Spanish invasion of Latin America. Although realising that this anniversary was really the 500th anniversary of the burning of the Library at Granada, the expulsion of the Jews from Spain and the quite appalling subjugation of other races, Cox decided to listen to what the producers had to offer.

They wanted him to direct a film based on a story by the Argentinean writer Jorge Luis Borges, and presented him with a list of the stories they had the rights to. Cox read them all and was first struck by Emma Zunz, the story of a woman who works in an oppressive factory and takes revenge on the evil owner, murdering him after pretending he has raped her. Kathy Burke would have had the lead role, but in the event, Cox decided on another story, *Death and the Compass*. This was a more straightforward thriller with a geographical twist to a series of murders.

Cox wrote the script, an odd tale of conspiracy in which a series of murders may or may not be motivated by the occult. The philosophical detective Lonnrot meditates and plays chess but must also deal with the underground rebel leader Red Scharlach and untrustworthy subordinate Treviranus, in a city torn by civil unrest. Nobody is

innocent in *Death and the Compass* and everybody is guilty of something. The story is portrayed as if it were the last in a long series of Lonnrot stories. But this is not Sherlock Holmes. Cox's script was so complex and bizarre that it frustrated the producers who began to get cold feet. They didn't understand it. After all, Cox had prepared a piece of pure entertainment that wasn't really about anything and the producers couldn't figure that out.

Cox knew what he had to do. He called the suits at the BBC: "It's about the contemplation of the void and Eastern mysticism and Buddhism combined with elements of Westernism and the Kabbala." It worked. They bought this elaborate explanation and contracts were drawn up and signed. Using the same crew he had just worked with on *Highway Patrolman*, Cox made the 55-minute film of *Death and the Compass* in Mexico City. The film stars three extraordinary actors. Peter Boyle plays Lonnrot, Miguel Sandoval plays the duplicitous Police Commissioner and Christopher Eccelston is the arch criminal Red Scharlach. Among the supporting cast are Pedro Armendariz Jr, Zaide Silvia Gutierrez and Alonzo Echanove.

The 55-minute BBC film aired in August 1992, to much critical acclaim: "Alex Cox's fantastic and witty film is fresh and bizarre...took the breath away." *The Times*. "Cox's work is so dreamily strange and compelling, so dark and cloistered in some parts, sexy, funny and exotic in others, that you wonder why no one has tried this before." *Time Out*.

However, the original story by Borges is a very literary piece and implies a long history of rivalry between Lonnrot and Red Scharlach. This is just assumed at the beginning of the story, which Cox had followed closely. One of the more confusing aspects of the BBC film is the lack of understanding of why Lonnrot hates Red Scharlach so much. Cox decided he wanted to expand on the 55-minute version and turn *Death and the Compass* into a feature film, so he began thinking about how he could improve on the narrative coherence of the piece. Producer Karl H Braun came up with extra funding for Cox to return to Mexico to shoot the additional scenes. The money came from Kuniaki Negishi of Cable Hogue and Katsumi Ishikuma of PSC, Cox's Japanese production partners on *Highway Patrolman*.

In the theatrical version, a flashback sequence explains the fallout between Lonnrot and Red Scharlach. We see that during a daring robbery, Red Scharlach has killed a friend of Eric Lonnrot's, an invented character called Commander Borges, a blind policeman played by Cox. But Scharlach has reason to hate Lonnrot too, an old score dating back to the death of Scharlach's brother in a bar room shoot-out with the cops. Over the years, each man plots to catch the other. Finally, the mysterious murder of Dr Marcel Yarmolinsky at the third Talmudic Congress gives Lonnrot a clue which will lead him, with the help of the atheist reporter Zunz, to unravel the greatest mystery of all.

Miguel Sandoval was brought back as a much older Franz Treviranus, Lonnrot's ex-boss, to tell the story of the investigation and its strange conclusion. Once the commissioner of city police detectives, he is now an ancient and embittered hermit

A FILM BY ALEX COX

in a NIGHTMARE CITY
inhabited only by CRIMINALS and POLICE...
a mystic DETECTIVE finds a TOOL
to catch a VILLAINOUS OUTLAW.

JORGE LUIS BORGES'

DEATH AND THE COMPASS

ESTUDIOS CHURUBUSCO AZTECA PRESENT A XHB / PSC PRODUCTION IN ASSOCIATION WITH CABLE HOGUE A TOGETHER BROTHERS PICTURE PETER BOYLE CHRISTOPHER ECCLESTON MIGUEL SANDOVAL AS TREVIRANUS "DEATH AND THE COMPASS" PEDRO ARMENDARIZ JR. ZAIDE SILVIA GUTIERREZ CLAUDIA BECKER ROCCO GIOFFRE MANUELA LOAEZA MIGUEL GARZON CECILIA MONTIEL CARLOS PUENTE KUNIAKI NEGISHI PRAY FOR RAIN KATSUMI ISHIKUMA ALEX COX JORGE LUIS BORGES KARL H. BRAUN / LORENZO O'BRIEN ALEX COX

▲ Christopher Eccleston as Red Scharlach in *Death and the Compass*

living on the outskirts of the Nightmare city. Treviranus layers on the additional levels of complexity and treachery in which he has been involved throughout the years. The new 93-minute version of *Death and the Compass* also received support from critics after it played at festivals in 1996: "wraps itself in a cloak of beauty…the work of a talented visionary." Kevin Thomas, *Los Angeles Times*. "Hilarious…A free-standing, colour-coded comic horror movie…A gorgeous surrealist dream." Ella Taylor, *LA Weekly*.

The architecture of Mexico is astounding and the film used some of Mexico's most striking locations, both modern and ancient. The height and beauty of the buildings is incredible and production designer Cecilia Montiel used as much as she could from that range. The City Police Headquarters where Detective Lonnrot works is Mexico City's classic Palacio de Correos – the 'Post Office Palace'. Lonnrot receives an honorary degree in the deco Palace of Fine Arts; his best friend is murdered in the vast, abandoned concrete wilderness of the Tolteca Cement Factory. Meanwhile, his enemy Red Scharlach waits for him in the Escher-like courtyards of the Convent of San Ildefonso and in a crumbling hacienda in Hidalgo.

Cox and cinematographer Miguel Garzon expand on the long take style they used in *Highway Patrolman* and the editor Carlos Puente intercuts long single takes with jump-cut 'flash forwards'. The result is flashy, dazzling and stylish: an outrageous

Peter Boyle and Christopher Eccleston in *Death and the Compass*.

theatrical romp. Actor Peter Boyle admits that, at the time, Cox's way of filming was very frustrating for him:

> "He had a theory of continuous shooting so the camera was moving around non-stop while I had to play a guy with endless dialogue – incomprehensible, metaphysical mumbling! I had to keep my mouth moving while the camera revolved around me which was extremely difficult. It was a really tough shoot for me; I hadn't been well and hadn't been working much, so it was a real challenge. But Alex is a great character and I get a big kick out of working with him, so it was all worth it in the end. Although, to this day, I still can't tell you what that story was about. Someone will have to explain it to me!"

Boyle wasn't the only confused actor on set. Christopher Eccleston now admits he took the part of Red Scharlach for the wrong reasons:

> "I'd been so disappointed when Alex didn't direct *Let Him Have It* and was so grateful to him for giving me that career break that *Death and the Compass* was a job I did out of loyalty. What I never admitted to Alex was that Borges made me feel stupid. I found it very difficult and just didn't get it. Looking back, I think I was probably quite tricky for Alex because I didn't understand what we were doing! Alex is an intellectual. He's literate and informed whereas I'm more prosaic, so it was a struggle for me to understand what he wanted. I was still quite young and unsure about myself as an actor, although I did work as hard as I could for him. What I did enjoy was the long tracking shots. I remember Peter Boyle being concerned by them but I really liked that style. Alex seems to have a willingness to let actors and technicians work on the edge of chaos and by extension, the audience have to work.

From an accomplishment point of view, *Death and the Compass* is probably the most difficult film Cox has made. In an interview for his web page, he admitted he was pretty ignorant before embarking on the project, having only read a couple of Borges' stories:

"He's a marvellous writer, of course – extremely highly regarded in Latin America and Spain. In the US and Britain I've seen him called a 'cult' writer, which is very depressing – as if great literature were a 'cult' instead of a zenith to which all writers should aspire. He's certainly been largely ignored by the film business, but that's inevitable. Borges writing is great, but dark, cynical, pessimistic. He documents hopelessness and pessimism, the impossibility of change or escape, the inevitability of fate and violence... You could not make a Mel Gibson movie out of one of these stories, nor a Merchant Ivory film."

Transferring Borges to the screen is something very few film-makers have ever been able to do. He is a very complicated and mystical writer who called this story 'a nightmare' and Cox sets his tale of murder and revenge in a labyrinthine nightmare city, a menacing world punctuated with announcements like "City Police Detectives are reminded that the Torture Area is to be kept tidy at all times. Use of the Torture Area is a privilege, not a right. Your co-operation is appreciated."

Cox's own nightmarish world was influenced by David Butler's 1930 sci-fi movie, *Just Imagine* and there are certainly shades of Fritz Lang's *Metropolis* (1926). He wasn't a major Borges fan before taking on the project but had spoken to the expert on Borges and the cinema, Edgardo Cozarinsky, whose book *Urban Voodoo*, Bennie reads in his room at the Adelphi Hotel in Cox's latest film *Three Businessmen*.

"According to Edgardo, Borges wrote two original film synopses, *Invasion* and *The Others*, for the director Hugo Santiago; he also co-wrote the screenplays. *Invasion* was filmed in Argentina in 1968; *Les Autres* was filmed in France in 1973. Films based on Borges' stories include *Dias de Odio*, a 66-minute Argentinean film based on *Emma Zunz* and directed by Leoplodo Torre Nilsson in 1955; *El Hombre de la Esquina Rosada*, a 70-minute Argentinean film directed by Rene Mugica in 1961; *Emma Zunz*, a 54-minute French film directed by Alain Magrou in 1969; Bertolucci's *Spider's Stratagem* (based on *The Theme of the Traitor and the Hero*) – made in Italy in 1969; and Edgardo's *Guerreros y Cautivos* (1997).

There is even another version of *Death and the Compass*: a black and white short film directed by Paul Miller at the London Film School back in the far-off Seventies, and shot by Dave Bridges, later the cinematographer of *Walker*. Apparently, Nigel Hawthorne plays Lonnrot.

▲ The Villa Triste-Le-Roy, the convent of San Ildefonso, where Lonnrot finally meets Red Scharlach.

» *Death and the Compass* producer Karl H Braun seen opposite in Tonino Valerii's 1974 western *My Name is Nobody*.

DIARY OF ALEX COX – THE MAKING OF *DEATH AND THE COMPASS*

1991

23 Aug	Start writing script of *Death and the Compass* (end of fifth week of editing *El Patrullero*).
2 Sept	Finish first draft *Death and the Compass*.
4 Sept	Additional dialogue recording, Mexico City.
30 Sept	Begin Mix, Skywalker, Los Angeles.
15 Oct	Finish Mix, Skywalker.
18 Oct	Time picture with Miguel Garzon, FotoKem.
30 Oct	First Answer Print.
4 Nov	*El Patrullero* screens at Churubusco, Mexico City.
10 Nov	Finish 2nd Draft, *Death and the Compass*.
4 Dec	*El Patrullero* screens privately for the Noailles and their guests at the Fine Arts, Los Angeles.

1992

17 Jan	Meet Simon Curtis, BBC, re: *Death and the Compass*.
24 Jan	Meet Cecilie Brown, Enrique de las Casas, in Madrid, re: *Death and the Compass*.
28 Jan	Finish Third Draft.
31 Jan	To London; SC says *Death and the Compass* is "95% on."
10 Feb	To Mexico City, re: casting – Claudia Becker; production – Karl Braun, locations – Diego Sandoval.

2 Mar PRE-PRODUCTION BEGINS, MEXICO CITY.
10 Mar Meet Peter Boyle, New York.
30 Mar PRODUCTION WEEK ONE – Costume Meeting.
31 Mar Chris Eccleston arrives; read through.
1 Apr Shoot Video Scenes.
2 Apr Paint Shop.
3 Apr Lonnrot's Flat.
4 Apr Sando arrives.
6 Apr PRODCUTION WEEK TWO – City Police Headquarters – Treviranus' Office (Palacio de Correos).
7 Apr CPHQ – Exts & Ints.
8 Apr CPHQ – Labyrinth.
9 Apr CPHQ – Night (British General Election – Tories win again!).
10 Apr CPHQ – Night.
13 Apr WEEK THREE – Travel to Hidalgo – Railway Station, Canyon, Triste-le-Roy.
14 Apr Triste-le-Roy Exts. Return to Mexico City.
15 Apr Hotel du Nord.
16 Apr Hotel du Nord.
17 Apr Railway Tracks (originally scheduled for Metro Int.).
18 Apr Train Int.
20 Apr WEEK FOUR – Triste-le-Roy Int. (Convent of San Ildefonso).
21 Apr Triste-le-Roy Int.
22 Apr Triste-le-Roy Int.
23 Apr To Estudios America; Pre-light.
24 Apr Triste-le-Roy Circular Room (Estudios America).
25 Apr Triste-le-Roy Circular Room (Estudios America).
27 Apr WEEK FIVE – Calle Torbitt Ext. (Estudios America).
28 Apr Liverpool House Int. (Estudios America).
29 Apr Liverpool House Int., Ext. (Estudios America). The shoot wrapped at 0600 hrs, i.e. the morning of Thursday 30 Apr, with the scene in which Lonnrot and Treviranus walk down Calle Torbitt at dawn after the riot.
5 May I went to Seattle to view our black and white rushes at Alpha-Cine (there being no black & white lab in Mexico). The picture was cut by Carlos' Puente at Estudios Churubusco in Mexico City.
10 July We screened the first answer print in Mexico.
21 July John Crane graded the 55-min video version for the BBC.

1993

17 Jan Karl Braun proposed shooting additional scenes for a *Death and the Compass* feature version, with finance from PSC in Tokyo.
26 Mar I went to Mexico and started writing the additional scenes. (In many cases these were based on 'Memos from Treviranus' which I had provided the art department as set dressing items the previous year.)
26 Apr PRE-PRODUCTION BEGINS, MEXICO CITY

31 May	SHOOT – Used Money Repository (Cementos Tolteca).
1 June	Used Money Repository (Cementos Tolteca).
2 June	Casa de Treviranus, Int.
3 June	Casa de Treviranus, Int.
4 June	Casa de Treviranus, Trial of Treviranus. Carlos and I worked on the new picture cut but it became apparent that there were no additional funds for post-production.
13 Nov	We boxed up all the material and shut *Death and the Compass* operations down. (Except for the business part. Over the next three years Karl Braun, Lorenzo O'Brien and I had to sort out the rights aspect: the short story by Borges was owned by Andres Vicente Gomez in Madrid, who had to be persuaded to sign a contract with us for the feature version; the BBC owned and physically possessed the negative of the 55-minute cut; the Mexican and Japanese rights issues also had to be resolved.)
1996	
6 April	I met Carlos at Churubusco. We picked up where we had left off: Rocco Gioffre provided us with additional special effects sequences (fires, skeletons, spinning newspapers); Tom Richmond shot a title sequence in a Labyrinth (lit by Shaun Madigan); Victor Barragan mixed the finished film at Churubuso in July: we saw our first answer print at Churubusco in August.

Death and the Compass premiered at the Tokyo Film Festival on 2 October and played at the Vancouver Festival on 12 October. It played at the Santa Barbara Festival on 7 March 1997, at Guadalajara on 15 March and opened theatrically on 11 July at Laemmle's Music Hall in Los Angeles.

Having made two films in Mexico, Cox was really feeling at home there. He had escaped the conformity of Hollywood and the lack of opportunity in Britain and liked the way Mexican film-makers had managed to hold on to the traditional chain of command. They hadn't become perverted by big budgets or disruptions to the chain that money causes. Instead, a hierarchy still exists in which the director, rather than a 'star', is at the top of the tree.

Ironically, lack of funds meant that even though the extra 30 minutes of *Death and the Compass* had been shot in 1993, it couldn't be completed until a later date. The film had been shot but was in pieces, with negative in Mexico, at the BBC in London and at a laboratory in Seattle. There was no money left for Cox to edit the film.

In order to fund the completion of *Death and the Compass*, Cox began taking acting jobs. The Mexican director Arturo Ripstein asked him to act in a film called *La Reina de la Noche (Queen of the Night)*, the story of a doomed alcoholic nightclub singer. Cox played the lover of Blanca Guerra. Having originally taken the job for the money, knowing he had a commitment to finish *Death and the Compass*, he found that he had loved every minute of working as an actor, being able to take a back seat for the first time in his career.

In 1995, Cox helped the Mexican producers promote Ripstein's film at Cannes. While he was there, he was approached by some American film producers who wanted him to direct a picture about gambling in the seamier edges of Las Vegas. The script by Wendy Riss was based on her own play *A Darker Purpose*. After reading it, Cox was tempted. He had never worked as a director-for-hire before but still needed the cash for *Death and the Compass*. He signed the contract. Now he was an employee.

The film was doomed from the word go. The producers immediately changed the title to *The Winner*, a move Cox knew would leave it open to every tabloid pun in the book. By calling the film *The Winner*, they were guaranteed reviews under headlines such as 'The Winner isn't' or 'The Winner is a loser', regardless of what the film was really like. "It's a disease among film reviewers, especially in Britain," explains Cox.

The production company was MDP Worldwide, a foreign sales company. A company like this works by making foreign sales projections, researching or guessing how much money they can make off the picture from international distribution. That means the casting comes down to 'the list' that everybody in Hollywood carries around with them. The list shows how much actors are worth in foreign sales, with the maximum score of 100 for people like Tom Cruise or Arnold Schwarzenegger. Many actors who happen to be household names in America still don't make it on to the list because they aren't recognised elsewhere. MDP were picking actors based on this list which meant Cox would be working with people like Michael Madsen and Vincent D'Onofrio. However, it also meant that the producers weren't thinking about the film as a whole. The five main actors were white. Cox demanded a person of colour and got Delroy Lindo, a very interesting actor who he was pleased to be working with.

Set in a rundown casino called Pair-a-Dice, outside mainstream Las Vegas, the characters are the kind of people who don't visit the main strip. To create the right ambience, production designer Cecilia Montiel needed the casino to be quite small: "We shot all of the interior of the casino in an old movie theatre called The Tower in Los Angeles. Architecturally, it was very stylish and very Baroque."

Everyman gambler Philip (Vincent D'Onofrio) is pulled from the brink of suicide after suddenly finding a winning streak on the roulette wheel. Everyone wants a piece of the action, including Louise (Rebecca DeMornay) a crass lounge singer who owes a lot of money to the casino owner Kingman (Delroy Lindo). Other distractions include Philip's brother Wolf (Michael Madsen), eccentric thug Joey (Frank Whaley) and Louise's partner in crime Jack (Billy Bob Thornton). Various Coxisms are on show, including the surreal Western landscape and a glowing chip Philip plays in the film's finale.

Without giving too much away, Cox has made it clear that he believes it wasn't a good idea to have the star of the film (Rebecca DeMornay) as executive producer:

▲ Cecilia Montiel, Cox's regular production designer, conceived the set design for *Mask of Zorro,* which Cox describes as 'a triumph of production design'.

"It's good for an actor to have a lot to say about what they do on set and how they are going to play the role but they should not have any power beyond that. It's not good for them to be able to sit down with the producers and re-cut the film or change the music."

Cox delivered the best version he could based on the material. He was paid his wage and immediately left for Mexico City to finish editing *Death and the Compass*. Unfortunately, while he was back in Mexico, the producers began to meddle. Pray for Rain's ironic score was completely cut and replaced with a very bland sound, described by Cox as "like fake jazz, of the kind they buy by the yard for pornos." Scenes were also cut, including a lot of very funny material with Delroy Lindo, Billy Bob Thornton, Michael Madsen and Frank Whaley.

Cox had originally created a counterpoint to the usual Las Vegas Hollywood

▲ Rebeeca DeMornay as Louise and Michael Madsen as Wolf in *The Winner*.

movies. Dan Wool of Pray For Rain knew that for the score, Cox wanted a certain feeling which wasn't reflected in the script:

> "Wendy Riss had written a very noir, Tarentino-esque thing and Alex isn't into any of those things and so he really wanted to go against them. The scores we do for him always add a counterpoint, so the reason it didn't work for the producers and distributors was because it wasn't a 'proper' Las Vegas score. It was an ironic score. It's part of Alex's way to go against convention like when he puts Joe Strummer's salsa music over the action sequences in *Walker*. He does it in imagery as well, like putting kittens in a punk rock club!"

» Star of the show, Rebecca DeMornay aka executive producer for *The Winner*.

Wool had undercut the sentimental moments in *The Winner* with screeching violins and kazoos, adding an extra hokey dimension to the film. The producers, however, were

obviously not quite as in tune with the Cox style in the way Wool was, a fact which doesn't surprise Cox's regular producer, Lorenzo O'Brien:

> "I saw Alex's cut which is a much better film. The studio took the edge out of it. If you hire an auteur to make a film, you expect an auteur piece. If you don't want an auteur piece, don't hire an auteur. It's very simple but I guess some people are too dense to understand that concept."

Cox's original cut was shown exclusively in Japan, but in Europe and North America, the only version available is the re-edited studio version. Cox has since been trying to remove his name from this picture: "The studio film is definitely not my movie. It's an Alan Smithee film."

Still in Mexico, after the fiasco of *The Winner*, Cox was offered another acting job. The Spanish director Alex de la Iglesia wanted him to play the town drunk in his film *Perdita Durango*. Not wanting to be covered in slime and vomit, Cox pushed for something more upstanding and took the role of a Mormon policeman instead. He played opposite the great American actor James Gandolfini as his sidekick. The film began shooting in Mexico and by the summer of 1996, ended up in Las Vegas...

Chapter Seven

No fear

What I'm talking about is money.
That's what it's all about.
I'm dealing with a product that costs several million dollars.
When you are dealing in millions,
you're dealing with people at their meanest.

Sam Peckinpah

Hunter S Thompson's 1971 countercultural book *Fear and Loathing in Las Vegas* has proven highly difficult to translate to the big screen. The self-described antics of the gonzo journalist would be a lot to ask of any writer–director.

Where the Buffalo Roam, starring Bill Murray as Thompson, opened in theatres in 1980 to universally bad reviews. It wasn't until more than a decade had passed until any firm new plans emerged for turning Thompson's book into a film. In 1992, producers Stephen Nemeth and Harold Bronson decided they wanted to make it as the first film for the newly formed company Rhino Films.

After two years of negotiations, in 1994, Nemeth finally made a deal with Thompson, his associate Laila Nabulsi and John Jergens of the Jergens Lotion dynasty, who was representing Shark Productions, a partial rights-holder. The budget was set at $5 million and the search was on for a script and a director. However, Rhino Films were going to lose the rights to the film if they didn't start shooting by January 1997. By October 1996, there was still no script and no pre-production. With only two months to find their script, things were getting tight.

Early names had included Jeff Stein, a well-known director of music videos, and

Cuban director Leon Ichaso (*Sugar Hill*). However, Laila Nabulsi had her sights set on either Lee Tamahori (*Once Were Warriors*) or Alex Cox. Tamahori and his writing partner flew out to Aspen to meet Thompson, but they soon fell out.

Cox was hired to direct and write the script. He developed the screenplay with his partner, Tod Davies who had already taught Hunter S Thompson's book while a professor at UCLA and, with Cox, had already thought a lot about what kind of movie it would make. While the script was being written, actors being considered included Keanu Reeves and John Cusack (who had directed a stage version of *Fear and Loathing* in Chicago). Benicio Del Torro (*The Usual Suspects*) was chosen for the role of Dr Gonzo. The film was to have been shot by Tom Richmond with Dan Bishop designing and costume design by Durinda Wood. However, the producers, who were very inexperienced, had made the mistake of offering the part of Raoul Duke to two different actors, John Cusack and Johnny Depp, at the same time. At this point, Cox realised that not only did they want a director signed up because they were in a hurry to get the film going, but they also needed somebody to sort out the actor problem they had created for themselves. Cox became the stalking horse for that negotiation.

A meeting with Hunter S Thompson was arranged. Cox and Davies travelled to Aspen to meet the great man. They were to meet him at the airport. He didn't show up. When they arrived at their hotel, a message had been left telling them to meet him at a bar that evening at 10pm. Thinking it would be some sort of dive bar where they could sit and talk about the project, they turned up to find the exact opposite. The bar turned out to be one of the most trendy, upmarket places in town with a queue of people desperate to get in to see a secret show by Lyle Lovett. They could only get inside if their name was on a list. The bouncer outside the club was extremely hostile and Cox and Davies were turned away. On their way back to the hotel, Davies turned to Cox: "Hunter's name was on the list, but maybe we should have checked to see if he'd put our names on the list." Cox looked at his partner knowingly and replied, "Tod, what you'll learn is that I am never on the list!"

Back at the hotel, after numerous attempts, Cox managed to track down Thompson by telephone: "I'll meet you at 2am," said Thompson. Having been up since five in the morning, Cox refused and immediately offended the great magnate.

The next morning, they awoke to discover a series of entertaining and expletive-filled messages on the machine. He had invited them to his secluded house that morning to watch football games, something neither Cox nor Davies was interested in, having travelled from Los Angeles in the hope of actually talking about the *Fear and Loathing* project. The author left a bloodstained blow-up sex doll near the side of the road to mark the turning to his house. Cox and Davies walked in to find Thompson with his videographer. Thompson is constantly videoed. Someone is making a video record of his life, something Cox found slightly odd.

> "When they weren't watching football, they'd put old videos of dinners held in his honour. It's a deeply

> pathetic scenario really. If he coughs, he insists the video is turned off because he doesn't want to be seen looking weak. And his head is in a bucket of alcohol. From about 10 in the morning he has a big beaker full of ice cubes and cheap liquor. Then he'd go off in his car and come back claiming he'd driven at a 100 mph. All we could do was just say, "I bet that was fun for you." It was if he was so desperate to impress us. But what is really worrying is that he is suffering. He is in a really bad way. Even though he has all these pilgrims and admirers going over there to tell him how great he is, the guy needs to check into a hospital. He's an alcoholic and he needs to get better. He needs to recover in the same way Dennis Hopper did. Dennis came to a point when he realised his life was going to hell and his work was suffering. Hunter Thompson hasn't come to that realisation. It's too bad because he was a great writer and the worst thing for a writer is to not write."

During the bad trip in Aspen, a strong feeling began to emerge that they had been set up. Davies believes they were supposed to have a quarrel with Thompson because of the money issue. Cox was used as a threat to Thompson. By sending him out to meet Thompson in Aspen, it was sending a message to the author that the producers were deadly serious about doing a low-budget movie, even though in hindsight they probably were not. A low budget meant a relatively small percentage cut for Thompson. On the other hand, if Thompson fell out with Cox, it would leave the way for more negotiations, in Rhino's favour, leading to a big-budget movie. The bigger the budget, the bigger the percentage everybody gets. Cox was the bargaining chip.

The official line is that Thompson didn't like their screenplay, but Davies says he hadn't even read the script:

> "He kept sitting there all morning trying to read the first three pages, then get another drink and say, "Let's do some acid!". We'd say, "Thanks so much Doctor Thompson but not today!" Then he'd try to bully us into bet on the football game. Alex would sit quietly saying, "Fine, I'll bet $10." Then he says to me, "You've gotta bet too!" So I say, "Fine, I bet $100 that in the next 10 minutes a man dressed in an animal outfit will run on to the field." So he called me a bitch! If he didn't want my point of view, he shouldn't have asked for it. Up until that

point, he had been largely ignoring Alex and would instead talk to me and keep pinching my hip, which I found very obnoxious. It was like going to visit the alcoholic family member's place at Thanksgiving and feeling you have to sit with them and get through it. We were expecting a real larger-than-life character but what we got was everybody's alcoholic uncle, and you can predict exactly what will happen. He'll drink; he'll start repeating himself somewhere around noon; he'll get angry if you don't give the right response; he'll have to eat something greasy in the afternoon to recharge; then around five or six in the afternoon, he'll have a sugar crash, completely lose it and explode for no real reason. I knew it was going to happen when his assistant disappeared. She obviously saw the clouds forming, knew it was coming and had got right out of the way. We had put one tiny animation scene in the middle of the script. A producer had told him about it before we arrived and she hadn't liked this Ralph Steadman cartoon. Hunter used this during his afternoon sugar rush and starting obsessing about the scene, even though he hadn't even read it. We were very calm and told him that if he didn't like it we would throw it out of the script. We would go as far as telling him we would be happy to do whatever he liked, but he still wouldn't stop yelling because he was somehow trying to manufacture an argument. Alex mentioned that if he didn't like the Steadman cartoons in the book, he should have got rid of them a long time ago, but he just ranted about how much he hated Steadman and shouted, "Let Steadman make his own movie!" Alex, I think, was expecting this kind of situation but, for me, it was absolutely crushing. He was a writer I had admired so much and was thrilled at the idea of meeting him but by the end of that day I was seriously depressed."

Next, enter Universal Studios, with their offer of a budget of $17 million and a deal with Rhino to distribute the film. At that point, Cox realised that the producers had always been pushing for a big budget Hollywood movie all along. Once he had got them the cast, they had their chance. They had realised their dream and could take their film to a major studio: "I doubt they ever really wanted to go the low road, which is unfortunate, since that was what the book clearly needed."

« Ready to write. Johnny Depp as Raoul Duke.

▲ Johnny Depp and Benicio Del Toro in *Fear and Loathing in Las Vegas*.

But in the pursuit of a bigger budget, the power had shifted from the director and the producers to the actors and their agents, and the inevitable uncertainty had descended.

Not surprisingly, Cox walked from the project. His exit from the film was, in part, due to the meeting with Hunter S Thompson but also to the fact Universal had become involved. Having befriended Hunter S Thompson, Johnny Depp stayed. After all, Universal was about to spend more millions of dollars marketing him. At the very least, the final production cost $20 million. Now, all the hype suggests the film cost a total of around $40 million. There is a certain irony about this, since the film was supposed to be a criticism of consumer culture.

Patrick Wachsburger at Summit Entertainment, Rhino's foreign sales agent, brought in Terry Gilliam (*Brazil* and *12 Monkeys*) as director. Gilliam claimed he didn't like the script written by Cox and Davies, and even told reporters that Cox had "managed to alienate everyone involved by deciding he could improve upon Hunter's work." There is something slightly disturbing about these remarks, because the quotes seem so over the top and removed from reality. Gilliam sounds as if he has been driven mad by the whole process.

It was reported that Gilliam, together with his writing partner Tony Grisoni, had written a new script, from scratch. Davies thought this to be reasonable and looked forward to seeing it:

"It was a great pleasure to work on the *Fear and Loathing* adaptation and a tremendously satisfying piece of writing to do; to feel that you had remained faithful to the book by solving the problem of translating Hunter's very strong individual voice into dramatic form. Nevertheless, Terry Gilliam has a very individual vision and we were looking forward to seeing his own script which we thought would be different and interesting, with a new perspective from ours in working from the book."

However, after Cox and Davies read the 'new' script, they found that at least the first 36 pages were remarkably similar and, in this section, their original structure was followed exactly. Even more frustrating was the ending of Gilliam and Grisoni's final shooting script. With regard to their own script, Cox and Davies had regarded as their single greatest contribution to the project, a restructuring of the end of Thompson's book. They had moved a short scene, set in a Hardware Barn, which was originally near the middle of the book. In their script, this place represents the real American dream that Duke is in search of – but he misses it. He has become hardened and crazed to the culture he so brilliantly criticises. He realises this for a moment and both feels defensively superior to the culture he fears and loathes, while obscurely knows

▼ The drugs don't work.

that he, at the bottom, is the same. This moral climax to the film is completely the invention of Alex Cox and Tod Davies. This is not the ending in the original book. For the final shooting script, Gilliam and Grisoni use Cox and Davies' exact scenario, but make it even more explicit. The invented character of the Proprietor's Daughter had been changed to his granddaughter, but the intent, the movement, and Duke's sense of shame – none of this to be seen in the original book – remains identical. At the end, the original book leaves Duke not on the open road but in Denver Airport, setting off on foot to buy a vicious dog. Ending the story on the open road, in the convertible, is the invention of Cox and Davies, as seen in their original draft, and subsequently copied in the final shooting script. There are many more incidents and scene descriptions, invented by Cox and Davies, as seen in their original drafts three (early 1997, D3) and two (late 1996, D2), which are incorporated into the final shooting script (FSS). Some examples are reprinted here but the full documentation is available for all to see at Katsumi Ishikuma's Alex Cox website located at www.pfcweb.com.

Page 1, Scenes 1.2

FSS:	D3:
Black screen, Dr Johnson quote, DUKE V/O	Black screen, Dr Johnson quote, DUKE V/O
FSS:	**D3:**
AAARRRGGHH!!! A red Chevy convertible - The Red Shark - wipes the black screen... The Red Shark races down the desert highway at a hundred miles per hour.	WHOOSH! The BLACK SCREEN gets wiped away by the WHITE DESERT and the RED CHEVY CONVERTIBLE that races down the highway at a hundred miles an hour...
FSS:	**D3:**
ON THE ROAD TO LAS VEGAS... AT THE WHEEL Strangely still and tense, RAOUL DUKE drives - skeletal, beer in hand - stares straight ahead... DUKE V/O I remember saying something like: I feel a bit light-headed. Maybe you should drive.	ON THE ROAD TO LAS VEGAS... AT THE WHEEL RAOUL DUKE, aka HUNTER S. THOMPSON, skeletal, bald, sunglassed, beer in hand... DUKE V/O I remember saying something like: "I feel a bit light-headed. Maybe you should drive..." ...DUKE stares straight ahead.

Page 2, Scene 2

FSS:	D3:
The sudden wrench makes GONZO nick his face with his razor.	DR. GONZO...SHAVES as they drive. Oblivious to the bloody NICKS this procedure has left behind.

(NOTE - the invention of Cox and Davies. No mention of blood nicks in original book)

FSS:	D3:
DUKE hops out of car... frantically opens the trunk to reveal what looks like A MOBILE POLICE NARCOTICS LAB.	He gets out of the car, goes to the trunk, OPENS it. IN THE TRUNK - a heavy drug and drink inventory. Like a mobile police narcotics lab.

(NOTE - D3 invention - in the original book, DUKE does not get out of car to open trunk)

==

Page 3, scene 3

FSS:	D3:
GONZO Let's give that boy a lift. GONZO wrenches the wheel - the RED SHARK swerves to the side of the road. DUKE We can't stop here - this is bat country!	DR. GONZO Let's give this boy a lift. DUKE We can't stop here! This is bat country! DR. GONZO grabs the steering wheel. The car swerves to the shoulder.

(NOTE - an adaptation by Cox and Davies. In original book, hitchhiker is picked up on Page 5; "This is bat country" line is on Page 18)

Page 9, Scene 8b

FSS:	D3:
The PINTO skids to a halt outside Polynesian bar, the black window full of Hawaiian shirts.	The PINTO parked haphazardly outside, a BUNCH OF BRIGHTLY COLORED SHIRTS hanging in the rear window.

(NOTE - No reference to shirts hanging in the back window of car in the original book - completely the invention of Cox and Davies)

==

Page 11, Scene 14

FSS:	D3:
EXT RUNDOWN BEACH HOUSE NIGHT...moonlight...	RUNDOWN BEACH HOUSE EXT NIGHT...moonlight...

(NOTE - There is no 'Rundown Beach House' in the book. It and the reference to a moonlit night are inventions of Cox and Davies)

==

Page 18, Scene 20

FSS:	D3:
A GROUP OF REPTILES at a table across the room stares at them, BLOOD DRIPPING FROM THEIR FANGS.	A GROUP OF REPTILES AT THE REGISTRATION DESK stares at them, blood dripping from their fangs.

(NOTE - Cox and Davies' original scene description. The book reads: "I pointed across the room to a group that seemed to be staring at us."

Page 25.)Page 19, Scene 21

FSS:

INT MINT HOTEL SUITE DUSK
A television shows the nightly news. A BUDDHIST MONK, protesting the war, sets himself on fire.

D3:

MINT HOTEL SUITE INT DUSK
DR. GONZO turns on the TV. The NIGHTLY NEWS, A BUDDHIST MONK, protesting the war, sets himself on fire.

(NOTE - Cox and Davies' invention and exact wording. No reference to BUDDHIST MONK protesting war or burning himself in the original book)

« Caught in a bad trip.

Page 61, Scene 76

FSS:	D3:
DUKE gives the POLICE CHIEF a polite smile - crosses to the elevator - turns to face the GAWPING COPS - pops a can of beer and toasts them. The doors close.	The POLICE CHIEF CROWD stare at him in shock as he waits by the ELEVATOR... DUKE gives a loud SNUFFLE, wipes his nose with his fingers, hauls another BEER out and opens it... DUKE gives them a friendly wave with the beer can, disappears into the elevator.

(NOTE - the elevator and salutation are completely the invention of Cox and Davies. In the book there is no elevator and no beer)

==

Page 65, scene 80

FSS:	D3:
DUKE	DUKE
Hotel Americana? I need a reservation. For my niece. Listen, I need her treated very gently. She's an artist, and might seem a trifle high-strung.	Hotel Americana? I need a reservation. For my niece. Listen, I need her treated very gently. She's an artist, and might seem a trifle high-strung.

(NOTE - FSS dialogue is identical to D3 dialogue. Original book is reported in the past tense - pp 118-119)

==

Page 65, scene 82

FSS:	D3:
EXT ON THE STREETS, A CAB STAND DUSK. The WHITE WHALE pulls up - DUKE at wheel. GONZO helps LUCY and her paintings from the car.	ON THE STREETS, A CAB STAND EXT NIGHT. The WHITE WHALE pulls up, with DUKE at the wheel. GONZO helps LUCY from the car into a CAB.

(NOTE - This location is the invention of Cox and Davies. In the original book, LUCY is abandoned at the airport. p119)

…and so it continues. These are simply a handful of examples of how numerous incidents and scene descriptions from Cox and Davies' original drafts have been incorporated in the final shooting script, clearing making a mockery of Gilliam's claim that he "only used two scenes".

After reading the final shooting script, Davies called Cox, believing Gilliam had used their own script on purpose to throw them the credit:

> "It was so blatant, I thought he used our script to make the producers angry for some reason. Gilliam and Grisoni literally must have put the script on a disk, put it in their computer and typed over it. Do they not remember doing that? There is too much internal evidence that shows they did that. Unless it's the most incredible channelling job in the history of screenwriting!"

The Writers' Guild of America (WGA) automatically arbitrates when a director claims screenwriting credit. The arbiters ruled in Davies and Cox's favour, concluding that they should get sole credit. This upset Gilliam, who threatened to resign from the WGA, and also upset the studio. The producers had the arbitration re-opened and, after much lobbying, managed to get Gilliam and Grisoni's names added to the writing credits, with a bitter Gilliam claiming he'd had to "fight with deranged egos." In relation to Cox's meeting with Hunter S Thompson, Gilliam had already claimed that Cox, "went up to his house and completely alienated Hunter in one fell swoop."

Tod Davies has one theory as to why the ex-Monty Python star had turned on fellow artists:

> "He had no other outlet for a person to get angry at where there wouldn't be immediate revenge taken. He couldn't get angry at Hunter S Thompson; he couldn't get angry at the producers or the actors; we were it, because we were on the outside. It was so inappropriate and such an explosion. The only other thing I could think of was that the whole process of directing *Fear and Loathing in Las Vegas* had driven him temporarily insane. This is a problem I have a lot of sympathy for because I really thought it might have happened to me and Alex if we'd stayed on much longer!"

Cox has another theory. He has been in the position of working for studios and knows the pressures of that environment.

> "I think there is a tendency on the part of directors to sometimes go a bit nuts and to try to get all the credits they

can. It is because many directors working for a studio feel their position is insecure. This is understandable because their job really is insecure. Therefore, they feel they need to triumph where they can. They are subordinate to the actors and so they have to try and beat the writer as their reward. What's the big deal? They already get to be director. Isn't that enough?

"It's a weird anxiety thing. It happened with Orson Welles and Herman J Mankiewicz in *Citizen Kane*. Maybe the director does this because he feels frustrated by the studio and the power of the stars.

"In my experience, having done *The Winner* and part of *Let Him Have It*, working 'for hire' is not a satisfactory experience because the director needs to be in charge if the film is going to be any good. Once you get into a situation where the actor or the producer is calling the shots, they become the author of the film rather than the director. In that situation, the director is just an employee with no job security. You can't be a maverick if you're directing a movie with Brad Pitt or Johnny Depp, because they call the shots. I feel sorry for Terry Gilliam because he was just working for a studio and he would have been constantly anxiety-filled. If he puts a foot wrong, he's out too and the studio replaces him with Peter Medak…or whoever. Directors, in a certain sense, become courtiers of movie stars. Everybody's waiting for the star to come out of the trailer. "Isn't he very well? We won't shoot today then. Oh, he wants to delay the film for six months? Okay we'll wait." But I don't want to be part of that process. If I'm going to make a film, I should be in charge of it, because if I'm not in charge, I can't do my job. My job is to make the film. It is not my job to appease some actor, but to give them advice and instructions as to how best to do the film."

After the first WGA arbitration ruling in Cox and Davies' favour, they received a call from Universal Pictures' lawyers who offered to pay them all of the money they owed them, both as writer and director, within 48 hours, on the condition they take their names off the picture. In effect, all they were offering was what was already owed to them – but within two days! Nearly 20 years ago, in Cox's student film, *Edge City*, the character he plays is in negotiations over a script and is told, "You know I never give advances in advance!" It never occurred to Cox that the industry really was as bad as this:

"Isn't it funny how you realise that all these things you cynically think are true when you're young turn

« Benicio Del Toro as Dr Gonzo.

out really to be true after bitter experience!"

At the time of writing this book, more than a year after Cox and Davies had started work on the *Fear and Loathing* project, they had yet to be paid.

Gilliam's film was booed at its premiere in Cannes and was slaughtered by critics. Around the same time, Hunter S Thompson made clear his own feelings about Gilliam, telling him,

> "You do not know me at all and you are not my friend. You are building a very distinguished enemies list, like Nixon."

At the *Fear and Loathing* premiere in New York, the stars turned out. The paparazzi got plenty of shots of Depp and Del Torro, either pictured with Gilliam or Thompson. Interestingly, there were no pictures taken of all four men together. While the film played, Gilliam retired to the bar. "I just want out of it," he said. So Gilliam seems happy to go along with (or be taken in by) stories that Cox 'alienated' Hunter S Thompson, but then after his own dealings with Thompson, describes him as a man who "behaves like an idiot and can't stop himself." Surely, through his own bitter experience, Gilliam can understand what really happened at the initial meeting between Cox and Thompson. Far from alienating the "Great Doctor", Cox spent most of the day declining his requests that they both do some acid.

When it became clear that Rhino were going to make the film of *Fear and Loathing in Las Vegas*, but not the right way, Cox and Davies pulled out and headed to Spain to further develop the Buñuel project. Sick of waiting around for vain glorious actors and unreliable producers, they decided they had to do something they could actually control.

Cox had been approached by the folk-punk band, the Levellers. Fans of his films and impressed by the music videos he'd made for the Pogues' *A Pair of Brown Eyes*, Joe Strummer's *Love Kills* and Debbie Harry and Iggy Pop's version of *Did You Ever?* (released as *Well Did You Evah!*), the Brighton band wanted Cox to direct the video for their next song *Too Real*.

Joe Strummer had once recorded a special piano solo for an earlier Levellers track, *Just the One*, and so Cox was interested in working with them:

> "The band's manager, Jonathan Bunney had also been sending me hand-written letters rather than phone, fax or e-mail, which I thought was unusual, and the band are really left wing and not afraid to take the piss out of themselves."

The Levellers were playing in Amsterdam so Cox went to Holland to meet them. He persuaded them to let him shoot the video in Liverpool. It was filmed in the style of Sixties' movies such as *The Thomas Crown Affair* and *Grand Prix*, using a split screen technique and featuring cameos from Margi Clark and Howard Marks. It plays on the idea of the band becoming a corporate organisation, interspersed with images of the Rolling Anarchy logo.

Cox had not worked in his home town since his days as a tape editor at BBC Radio Merseyside. *Too Real* was shot in August 1997 and was released as a single in March 1998. Making the video put Cox in touch with the Film and Television Commission for North West England and the Liverpool Film Office. Both organisations played a vital role in supporting Cox's next, and most recent production...

Chapter Eight

Life on the road

Modern bourgeois society, a society that has conjured up such gigantic means of production and exchange, is like the sorcerer who is no longer able to control the powers of the underworld that he has called up by his spells.
Communist Manifesto

You know, capitalism is above the law,
It say 'it don't count 'less it sells';
When it costs too much to build at home,
You just build it cheaper some place else.
Bob Dylan, 1983

In the 15 years since Alex Cox made *Repo Man*, the world has become a more dangerous and even more alienating place. Frightening, desperate, corporate-controlled, lonely…but is there any meaning behind the horrible facade? Cox prefers to laugh more than cry. Hence *Three Businessmen* – a comedy about serious things.

Three Businessmen is a one-of-a-kind movie that has some genuinely funny moments and a lot of very dark ones too. The Alex Cox penchant for off-the-wall characters and odd situations is very much in evidence. Fans of Cox's offbeat style will relish his familiar trademarks – long takes (this time he's down to only 102 cuts in the whole film), strange dialogue and quirky details. Tod Davies' tightly constructed, uncompromising script is philosophical without being too dry, entertaining as well as experimental. Davies is obviously influenced by art films such as Buñuel's *Discreet Charm of the Bourgeoisie*, Jean Renoir's *The Rules of the Game* and Ingmar Bergman's *Smiles of a Summer Night* and is convinced there is still a market for these kind of films.

Quite simply, *Three Businessmen* is the story of Bennie and Frank, two independent businessmen, who meet by chance in the restaurant of the Adelphi Hotel in Liverpool. Unable to find food therein, they tentatively join forces and set out in search of dinner, in a city neither of them knows. In the course of one night, their journey takes them from Liverpool to Rotterdam, Hong Kong, Tokyo and the desert, even though perhaps they don't realise it.

Cox plays Frank. With everyone working to a tight budget, it was useful to have Cox acting as well as directing. One less air fare and one less salary. But it's hard to believe this was the major deciding factor in having Cox play a lead role. He is perfect for the part and his real life insight into the themes involved is put across in a way not seen before. The subject matter of the script obviously means a lot to him. Certainly, it would be difficult to imagine more conventional actors trying to grasp the values and ideas being expressed in *Three Businessmen*. In addition, for Cox, as he mentions on his website, there is the revenge aspect:

> "One sees all these movie actors, often hugely wealthy already, friggin' millionaires, going to the studios and getting free money to direct their little first-time-director efforts. While workin' stiff directors are shivering beside freeway on-ramps, holding cardboard signs saying, 'Will Direct for Chardonnay'. It's sickening. From now on I will only cast directors: coming soon, my version of *Little Women* starring Arturo Ripstein and Arthur Penn. With Spike Lee as Beth.'

Bennie is played by Miguel Sandoval, his sixth collaboration with Cox. As well as Alex Cox projects such as *Repo Man*, *Walker* and *Death and the Compass*, Sandoval's other film credits include *Jurassic Park* and *Clear and Present Danger* as well as TV appearances in *Seinfeld* and *Frasier*. Having been involved in most of Cox's films, Sandoval has come to the conclusion Cox will never mellow:

> "He's always been extraordinarily independent-minded and anti-authoritarian. *Three Businessmen* is proof he hasn't wavered from that stance. In fact, he's become more belligerent as he's got older. The fact he hasn't become hugely wealthy or successful has earned him my respect. I've never known him to show one bit of regret or remorse for anything he's done. He will stick his feet down into the mud, even if he knows he's cutting off his nose to spite his face, just for the sake of doing it, and for the sake of saying "Guess what? I'm not going to do

▲ Miguel Sandoval as Bennie (left) and Alex Cox as Frank.

what you say!" He may even know that sometimes studio executives are correct – but he just doesn't care."

With *Three Businessmen*, there were no hassles from faceless executives. The film came about after Cox and Davies were approached by Dutch philosopher and bon vivant, Wim Kazyer, for a contribution to his television series on the theme of beauty and consolation. They were given carte blanche, with control over all aspects of the production: the script, the casting, the locations and the crew. Funding came from VPRO television in Holland, Film Funds Rotterdam and from Cox and Davies' own company, Exterminating Angel.

After the *Fear and Loathing* experience, and the much publicised dispute over writing credits for that film, Cox and Davies set up Exterminating Angel Productions as a direct result of that whole saga. Having also had to endure studio interference on the 1996 project *The Winner*, they were tired of the whole process of working for producers who didn't really know what kind of film they wanted to make. Now, through Exterminating Angel, with Davies as producer and Cox as director, they are in the position of working for themselves. There is a simple philosophy behind the set up. For Davies, the process of studios making big budget films over and over again is wasteful:

» On the road again in a scene from *Three Businessmen*.

"It should be possible to make a more manageable, lower budget film that you can then still make a profit on. Film-making shouldn't be an alienating process in which everybody's making a huge amount of money in exchange for the leaching away of all meaning out of their job."

Cox and Sandoval in the corporate road movie.

Three Businessmen is the start of an alternative way forward. Cox and Davies sacrificed a large amount of money for complete autonomy. They were the company so they could make decisions with crew members very quickly. There was therefore never a situation when they were moving in one direction with another faction moving against them. Everyone who was working on the film was working together because they weren't in it for money, or for power, but because they liked the project and wanted to push it forward. Cox and Davies had the opportunity to make a film with people they wanted to work with and about something they felt was interesting and important. On the surface, the film is about how friendship can be found in solitude, but on a deeper level, it is about the alienation of the modern world.

Bennie and Frank are two lone businessmen lost in the world. There's a sense of anxiety, of vulnerability and the drive to escape, but there's nobody to help. It is as if they are suffering from some sort of homelessness. But at the same time, these alienated individuals seem just about able to cope with environments, across all boundaries of geography. Cox presents a world of dissolving boundaries where any

▲ A comedy about serious things.

particular place no longer supports individual identity. Wherever we are, we live in a new disorientating global space. Is there any way out?

Dubbed "a corporate road movie" by *Variety*, *Three Businessmen* is a vision of a cold, impersonal world, a dystopian image of capitalist progress. Filtered through his trademark irony, Cox explores displacement and the subtle dangers of globalisation and literally shows us this global village created by international corporate capitalism. How much the boundaries of the nation have been transcended by advertising and flows of information and culture is striking. Independence and 'separateness' and therefore the power of the nation state has been eroded. In our karaoke culture, every new idea is copied. Global cultural patterns of consumerist ideology are emerging, which, so far, socialism has yet seriously to upset.

Three Businessmen is unpredictable, dislocating and somewhat disturbing. Wherever Frank and Bennie find themselves, the background still seems familiar, each place resembling the last. The neon lit cities of Liverpool, Rotterdam, Tokyo and Hong Kong are the same. As well as entertaining the audience, there is a certain mood conveyed. All is not well. We are not living in the best of all possible worlds. Cox shows the disorientating effects of Tokyo, a place where the line between the real and the simulated is completely blurred due to an artificial reality of karaoke, computer games and other high-tech experiences. Japan's

▲ Where are we now? Everywhere.

technological advancement is leading the world into the future, having transcended Western modernity, with global dominance in the image industries. Japan is no longer an exotic culture of Zen and Kabuki but one of virtual reality and simulation. Rotterdam, Hong Kong and even Liverpool are similarly de-centred cities. There is no longer any place like home. There is no home. We are unsettled, de-centred, in exile.

Three Businessmen is about the anxiety that globalisation produces. Bennie and Frank are hanging on by their fingernails, trying to keep their own centre. All they can do is talk gibberish, about safe subjects such as computers. This, according to Cox, is one of the reasons why the characters don't realise where they are.

> "They know that if they talk about computers, nobody will be offended. Bennie and Frank never really say anything that can provoke a strong reaction in the other character because we don't want to; we just want to get by. The last thing we want to do is have an argument or really address anything. At one point, Bennie wants to talk about sex, but Frank doesn't want to talk about that. We have so much to hide and so much to conceal. We are so

▲ Is there any way out?

withdrawn and protected. It was very important to me that the conversations were banal, as in Kubrick's *2001*, which was a big influence in our film. There are extraordinary events happening to the characters but they never address them. They only talk about cheese sandwiches. Incredible events are taking place such as the exploration of the planets and the discovery of another form of intelligence which has made us both intelligent and murderers. This isn't talked about. Instead, it's, "Are you going to be home for my birthday?" or "How's your lovely wife. We must get together for Thanksgiving."

"*2001* is such a great script, but even now it's not really thought of as a great script; it's thought of as a great special effects film. It seems weird that this huge film could be the inspiration for our little film, but it is. In *Three Businessmen*, the Adelphi Hotel is so like the end of *2001*, with that really mad hotel that the aliens have built for him in his mind.

> "The original idea was to make a film in the style of Buñuel. We were going to have two couples who go out for the evening and drive around the world without knowing it. They would drive through deserts, jungles and mountains without knowing where they are and never finding their final destination. After budgeting, it was found to be a very expensive idea, so we adapted the same theme and came up with *Three Businessmen* with the two guys walking around instead. Incidentally, the geography in Liverpool, Rotterdam and Hong Kong is feasible. Bennie and Frank walk in circles but it all connects together as it should."

The third businessman, Leroy, is played by Robert Wisdom (*Face Off* and *Mighty Joe Young*). He isn't introduced until near the end of the film, when Bennie and Frank find themselves in the desert. Up until this point, in every country, posters advertising some sort of rock star called Daddy Z have been present in the background, where ever the pair go. Symbolically, the Daddy Z fliers have represented the guiding star. The journey has been a symbolic one and the trip has highlighted their own loneliness and fear.

The film culminates in an odd take on the story of the Three Wise Men. Amidst an assortment of Christmas decorations, in a truly magical moment, the Magi gather around a crib to look at a new born baby. Finally, they are led out by a little girl – a little hand of God. As the credits roll, we hear Debbie Harry singing a techno version of *Ghost Riders in the Sky*.

Davies suggests that although an international culture has replaced national identities, with the beginning of a new millennium, alternative philosophies are emerging:

> "We're on the edge of something new. We're living in another Roman empire, where the empire has spread through the known world, which happens to be bigger now. On the edge of it, in an outcast group, is being born another possibility. It happened at the end of the Roman empire in Jerusalem and Bethlehem and it can happen again. People then were just getting on with their lives too, although they wouldn't have been talking about computers!"

For so long, it is as if there has been no competing ideologies with bland, centred politics and vacant lifestyles. As people get older, they tend to become more right wing, acquiring property and children. Subsequently, they come to want what is best for their kids rather than what is best for the whole of society. The massive corporatisation of the

▲ Alex Cox contemplating life.

world means that everybody is supposed to eat McDonalds, stay at the Hilton and go and see Mel Gibson movies. This means an increasing lack of questioning of the results of big business and globalisation and the inequality that goes with it. Cox doesn't opt for an easy life; he's still the radical he always was. For him, there is a regional solution:

> "Let's hope that in spite of the international global monolith and the neo-liberal experiment and the New Labour Party, in the end, regionalism will triumph and we'll nationalise the railways."

Three Businessmen was completed in the summer of 1998. Final cost? No man can say. Cox will not say because, when people work for the love of the project, it's difficult to put together a real cost. Most of the cast and crew worked for a tiny fraction of what they would normally earn, so if he confessed how much money was spent, it wouldn't be a fair reflection on what the film is actually worth. It would also be misleading because of the certain amount of luck involved along the way. Realistically, it would be impossible for the film to be made again in the future because it just so happened that a group of very talented people had gaps in their work schedule and could devote their time.

DIARY OF ALEX COX – THE MAKING OF *THREE BUSINESSMEN*

1998

2 Jan — Wim Kayzer of VPRO approved a faxed script and budget proposal Tod and I had made.

31 Jan — We arrived in Amsterdam and met him and his assistant Chris Williger to discuss the script. The following week we applied for a production loan from Dick Willemsen at Film Funds Rotterdam.

18 Feb — VPRO officially approved the budget of our project, tentatively titled *Dad Has Left The Building*.

20 Feb — First draft script complete.

9 Mar — Scout locations in Xochimilo, Mexico (ultimately not used).

16–19 Mar — Scout Tokyo locations with Katsumi Ishikuma and Chigumi Obayashi of PSC.

22 Mar — Tod and I to Liverpool; Meet Christine Colvin at office, FTC@NW.

24 Mar — Drew Schofield and John McMartin in *Dreams Of Children* at the Masque Theatre.

31 Mar — Director of Photography, Robert Tregenza arrives.

11 Apr — Sando arrives.

12 April — WEEK ONE
LIVERPOOL – DAY ONE
10. THE REVOLVING DOORS OF THE HOTEL – DUSK
11. IN THE HOTEL LOBBY
12. IN THE LIFT
20. FRONT LOBBY, HOTEL

13 April — LIVERPOOL – DAY TWO
17. FRENCH RESTAURANT – FOYER
18. IN THE RESTAURANT

14 April — LIVERPOOL – DAY THREE
2. ST GEORGE'S HALL
3. THE NORTHWESTERN HOTEL
4. LIME STREET STATION
5. INTO LIME STREET STATION
6. THE RAILWAY PLATFORM
7. THE STATION SHOPS
8. THE STREET – SNOWING
9. AT THE LINE OF CABS (HOTEL EXT.) – DUSK

15 April — LIVERPOOL – DAY FOUR
13. OUTSIDE THE LIFT – FIRST FLOOR
14. AT THE END OF THE HALL
15. IN ROOM 147
16. ROOM 147 – A MOMENT LATER
19. THE KITCHEN

16 April — LIVERPOOL – DAY FIVE
21. IN FRONT OF THE HOTEL
22. ACROSS THE STREET – LEWIS'S

	23. A STEAK RESTAURANT
	24. AT THE TURN TO MATHEW STREET
	25. IN FRONT OF GRAPES PUB
17 April	LIVERPOOL – DAY SIX
	26. AT THE PIER HEAD
	27. PIER HEAD – CAR SHOWROOMS
	28. BUS INT.
	32. OUTSIDE JAMES STREET STATION
	33. JAMES STREET STATION – PLATFORM
18 April	OFF
19 April	LIVERPOOL – DAY SEVEN
	29. ON THE STREET
	30. IN THE PUB
	31. THE STREET
20 April	WEEK TWO
	TRAVEL TO ROTTERDAM – DAY EIGHT
21 April	ROTTERDAM – DAY NINE
	34. ON THE TRAIN
	35. ON THE TRAIN
	36. BEURS STATION PLATFORM
	37. AT THE TOP OF THE ESCALATOR
22 April	ROTTERDAM – DAY 10
	39. INSIDE THE TRAMHUYS
23 April	ROTTERDAM – DAY 11
	40. ON THE STREET
	41. INSIDE THE PANOS GREEK RESTAURANT
	42. ONTO THE STREET
24 April	TRAVEL – DAY 12
	Meet ROBERT WISDOM; travel to DESERT
25 April	DESERT – OFF
26 April	WEEK THREE
	DESERT – DAY 13
	70. LOS ANGELES – IN A ROOM
	68. DESERT – DUSK FOR DAWN
	69. DESERT – PHONE BOOTH – DAWN
	71. DESERT – PHONE BOOTH – DAWN
	72. ACROSS THE DESERT – DAWN
	73. FARTHER ALONG ON THEIR TREK
	74. ON THE BACK OF THE WOODEN CART
27 April	DESERT – DAY 14
	76. AT THE EDGE OF A SMALL DESERT TOWN
	77. AT THE TOWN FOUNTAIN
	78. UP AHEAD
	79. DOWN THE STREET – A SIDEWALK FOOD STAND
	80. AT THE SIDEWALK STAND
	81. AT THE SIDEWALK STAND – LATER
	85. IN THE STREET
28 April	DESERT – DAY 15
	82. IN A PITCH BLACK HALLWAY
	83. INSIDE THE BACK ROOM
29 April	DESERT – OFF
30 April	TRAVEL – DAY 16
1 May	ROTTERDAM – DAY 17
	65. INT. TAXI BLUE SCREEN
	43. AROUND THE

	CORNER – A VAST PLAZA
	43A. MAIN STREET
2 May	ROTTERDAM – DAY 18
	44. ON THE TRAM
	45. THE STREET
	38. A STREET OF SHOPS
3 May	TRAVEL – DAY 19
4 May	WEEK FOUR
	ARRIVE HONG KONG – DAY 20
	47. HONG KONG HARBOUR
	48. ON THE STAR FERRY
5 May	HONG KONG – DAY 21
	49. AT THE STAR FERRY HARBOUR – KOWLOON SIDE
	50. UP THE STREET
	51. ON THE TRAM
6 May	TRAVEL & SCOUT TOKYO – DAY 22
	52. DOWN THE ALLEY
	53. IN SHINJUKU DISTRICT
	62. OUTSIDE BAR/RESTAURANT, OGIKUBO
	63. INSIDE BAR/RESTAURANT
	64. OUT ON THE STREET
7 May	TOKYO – DAY 23
	(No shoot due to inclement weather)
8 May	TOKYO – DAY 24
	60. UP A STAIRCASE
	61. ALONG OVERPASS
	58. UNDER RAILROAD, GINZA
	59. OUTSIDE A KARAOKE BAR
9 May	TOKYO – DAY 25
	54. OUTSIDE NOODLE SHOP
	55. INSIDE NOODLE SHOP
	56. OUTSIDE NOODLE SHOP
	57. INSIDE NOODLE SHOP
10 May	TRAVEL – DAY 26

All return to their appointed destinations.

On 19 May we screened rushes at Soho Images in London. Picture was edited, on a flatbed, in Rotterdam from 21 May to 16 June. Post-production sound was done in San Francisco, at Richard Beggs' studio and at Pray For Rain's headquarters.

The final mix was done by Richard at Skywalker in San Rafael in August; Adam Vardy shot an additional scene for us in New York on 22 September. The 35mm blow-up (from Super 16mm) was done by Frank Rizzo of Metropolis Labs in New York.

The first public screening of the film was at Channel 4 Television's headquarters in central London on 28th September, before the official world premier at the Hampton's Film Festival in New York on October 16th. However, the screening Cox was most nervous for was one in Liverpool in November:

▲ Alex Cox and co-star in Luis Estrada's *La Ley de Herodes*

"It's the home town and I knew I wouldn't be given any kind of break just because we'd shot part of the film in Liverpool. Film-makers shoot there all the time!"

Three Businessmen is independent film-making at its best. The film is intelligent, artistic, thought-provoking and, above all, different. Audiences will be challenged by it. Each will have their own opinion and participate in the formation of their own individual reading of the film. This enigmatic and extraordinary work is, hopefully, just the beginning. Simply to be able to pull off a film of this nature and concept is real evidence of Cox's talent as a film-maker.

The future looks bright. Cox still wants to make another film in Liverpool, probably an adaptation of *The Revenger's Tragedy*, based on a screenplay by Frank Cottrell Boyce. He also wants to make his film about the life of Luis Buñuel. It now looks likely to be made in Mexico, produced the Mexican way, which means it is will not be contingent on cast. Previously, it was to have been made based around an international stellar cast with the star's salaries much greater than the budget for the rest of the film. Cox has already been back to Mexico, in his role as actor, playing in Luis Estrada's *La Ley de Herodes* (*The Law of Herod*). He spent four weeks on location in

Tehuacan and in Mexico City, playing an obnoxious gringo, in a film in which almost everybody is really bad. Going back to work on Estrada's film reminded him of how much he loved the place and it is most likely most of the work Cox will be doing in the future will be based in Mexico.

La Ley de Herodes (*The Law of Herod*) played at the Acapulco Film Festival on 10th November to much controversy. IMCINE disowned the film and pulled it from the festival, the actors protested and forced it to be shown. It will be screened at the Sundance Film Festival this year and released in the UK as *Pigs Will Fly*.

"Mexico is so film-maker friendly and it's not about money. I am really only interested in making films. I'm not interested in making large amounts of money or in being highly regarded in the US. I think the British have a cultural problem because we share the same language as the Americans. We're inevitably trapped in this dance of death with the Americans and producing films which we think will make them happy. Loutish comedies, gangster films or old Jeeves the butler Merchant Ivory stuff. I hate all that. It's not about film-making, it's about producing acceptable pabulum.

"There was a guy in the assistant director's department on the production of *The Winner* who came up to me and said, "I wanna be just like you so I can make the big money." Of course, I had to tell him that to earn 'big money', you don't become the sort of director I am, you aim for the world of Hollywood, or become an actor.

"I'm serious. Don't go to film school or produce TV commercials: become an actor, better yet, a movie star. The way it works is this: in the old days, as long as you were British or Irish or Dutch, or sounded like you were, you could go into any studio in Hollywood and they'd throw a couple of pictures at you to direct, straight off, no problem.

"The problem was, this great generation of artisans, former directors of those fabulous Hovis commercials of our childhood, colluded with the studios in the monumental lie that making a movie costs $30, $40 or $50 million! What rubbish. And you're not seeing $50 million on the screen, either, even though you're paying for it, because the leading hunk is taking $10 million, the

director $2.5 million, the producer $3.5 million, and the studio is squeezing another $10 million in 'overheads'.

"The studios like to spend a lot of money on a product, because if you can convince people to push up their prices, films become more expensive and fewer films get made. And if the studios control the market – and in some cases they own the cinemas – it's in their interest to have less product on the market: they make the same money for fewer units moved!

"And who, ultimately, moves those units anyway? Is it the director? No. And there's the rub. Because it's actors who ultimately sell the product. Perhaps the best-selling actor of them all is Clint Eastwood.

"The studios want to keep film-making to a minimum: at the same time they wish to monopolise the talents of certain desirable actors. How did Warner Brothers make sure Clint Eastwood stayed with them, acting in cowboy and *Dirty Harry* films? 'Find out if Clint wants to direct something.' (Thinks: 'That'll keep him busy till we're ready for another *Dirty Harry*') 'He wants to act in his own movie? Sure, kid! Why dontcha! (Thinks: 'Straight to video.')

"What else could explain the proliferation of these actor–director sob stories and vanity trips? 'Hey man, you see the new masterpiece directed by Kevin Costner/ Jodie Foster/Sean Penn/Emilio Estevez/John Tuturro/ Keenan Wayans/Alan Alda/Leonard Nimoy/William Shatner/Lassie...?' It really is appalling.

"In the US, the movie stars call all the shots whereas the directors are mere employees. If you want to be a director in the idea of Buñuel or Kurosawa as directors, you can't look to the US for the resolution of your dreams. There's a certain romanticism that there are a few American directors who are rebels. Look at Kubrick. He spent nine years in pre-production on a film called *Artificial Intelligence*, written by Brian Aldiss. He lost his agent, Michael Ovitz who went to work for Disney. Ovitz says to him, 'Forget about *Artificial Intelligence*, you wanna do a film? Do *Eyes Wide Shut* – Tom Cruise, Nicole Kidman – I'll get you the gig. Here's the script.' Who has the power? Kubrick dragged

« Alex Cox and co-star in Luis Estrada's *La Ley de Herodes*

the process out endlessly and made it last two and half years but in the end, he was still an employee of the studio. He was the greatest living director and he never got to make the film he worked for nine years to do. He did the alternative film that the studio threw at him. It's sad to spend so much time struggling and then failing. But it's inevitable. Life can't be a string of victories. You have to do your best and be prepared to accept failure. There is ultimately no reason to worry, because, in the end, independent, personal films are the only ones that matter. They are the only ones that will be remembered, over time.

"Hollywood isn't really about films. It's about bureaucrats, and their fears, and their attempts to overcome their fears by subjugating others. In the film business, they talk about their love of movies and a desire to make great films in Hollywood. But they don't desire to make great films; they desire status and money in a fetid cesspool of second-rate ambition and mediocre aspirations. It's better to avoid that at all costs.

"The film that I made that lost the most money might be the best one, and one that made the most money might be the worst one. There is no corollary between money and quality. The Mexicans know that."

Cox doesn't go for the glory. He could have done that a long time ago. After *Repo Man* and *Sid & Nancy*, films that achieved much high praise from the critics, he didn't try to go all out to capitalise on this success with follow-up movies. Offers were coming in, such as *Robocop*, that would have taken him on a different path. But if he had signed up for those sort of projects, he would have had to live with himself! Instead, he has chosen to pursue personal films such as *Walker*, *Highway Patrolman* and *Three Businessmen*, projects without an obvious attraction for the mainstream audience and therefore incapable of finding funding from major studios. Cox is an auteur, writing as well as directing most of his material and prefers to work outside systems that threaten to impose controls during production. He has managed to enforce his own anarchic, absurdist vision of the world on a unique series of films.

Alex Cox still remains an outsider. The Hollywood film industry is now very much part of the global economy he critiqued in *Three Businessmen*, a world run by accountants, uptight sneaky men and women in Armani suits, constantly on their cellular phones. As an independent film-maker, Cox is no yes-man and can afford to keep his distance from those who 'do lunch'. Rather than consolidating success, he

IT'S EASY TO BE IN THE

MOVIES!

FAST MONEY!

$100'S

FOR DOING NOTHING!

Casting Company is looking to cast "extras" TODAY for current projects filming in L.A.! Everyone is welcome because we need all types for Movies, TV Shows, Commercials, and Music Videos. This is an easy way to get money, PLUS you make money when you want to, and you get to hang out with your favorite stars. Going to the set, is like going to a party! Full time, part time, spare time (weekends).

Making money shouldn't be this much fun!

CALL TODAY (818) 503-2362

Your Area Rep is: Nicole Moore
MAKE 100'S APPEARING IN - MOVIES/TV/VIDEOS
CALL TODAY (818) 503-2362

Your Area Rep is: Nicole Moore
MAKE 100'S APPEARING IN - MOVIES/TV/VIDEOS
CALL TODAY (818) 503-2362

Your Area Rep is: Nicole Moore
MAKE 100'S APPEARING IN - MOVIES/TV/VIDEOS
CALL TODAY (818) 503-2362

Your Area Rep is: Nicole Moore
MAKE 100'S APPEARING IN - MOVIES/TV/VIDEOS
CALL TODAY (818) 503-2362

Your Area Rep is: Nicole Moore
MAKE 100'S APPEARING IN - MOVIES/TV/VIDEOS
CALL TODAY (818) 503-2362

Your Area Rep is: Nicole Moore
MAKE 100'S APPEARING IN - MOVIES/TV/VIDEOS
CALL TODAY (818) 503-2362

Your Area Rep is: Nicole Moore
MAKE 100'S APPEARING IN - MOVIES/TV/VIDEOS
CALL TODAY (818) 503-2362

moves on immediately, getting involved in increasingly ambitious and challenging projects. He has tried to put a new spin on existing formulas and genres and so as a writer and director Cox is forever producing truly original work. The only problem with his anarchic style of genre-busting is that his films aren't part of a consistent body of work. Audiences like to know what to expect. With Cox, they are always challenged. If he would only keep making films about young punks in Los Angeles, there wouldn't be a problem. By now, we'd all have seen *Repo Man 7*. After *Sid & Nancy*, Cox was asked to direct both *Needle* by Jimmy McGovern and *The Basketball Diaries*, but he was sick of junkies. He doesn't want to have a career as the director of junkie-themed films or rock and roll-themed films. He was also offered *Natural Born Killers*, but isn't interested in violence or action sequences for their own sake. Therefore, because everything is new or slightly different, it's harder for the audience. If they come looking for another flying car, they'll be disappointed.

Having rejected the dead-end streets of Hollywood, Cox now lives in Oregon, but will continue to travel. Flitting between Mexico, LA, Almería, London, Liverpool and wherever future projects will take him, he is always busy, usually thinking and talking about movies; researching and developing new ideas. And most importantly, he's making the films he wants to make. Quite simply, he has no regrets, proof – were any needed – that he has not changed. With both the will and strength to follow his own individuality, he has rejected the rules, refused to play the game and always lived his own way. Given the dictates of modern Hollywood, Alex Cox will never play the game, but will always buck the system. His films will continue to resist categorisation. Don't expect a linear narrative. Expect extraordinary performances within cinematic chaos.

So far, Cox has made some of the great movies of the last two decades. But, as with many directors of his calibre, this has yet to be fully acknowledged. At the moment, film-makers like Alex Cox find it difficult to compete with the mass of Hollywood blandies for recognition. They have the financing and the marketing money for their guaranteed money-spinners. But for all the hype, in a hundred years from now, it won't be today's monotonous mainstream garbage that people will be watching.

In the meantime, take a look at one highly dedicated film-maker and wonder: where will this anarchist lead us next?

Chapter Nine

Filmography

As an actor, Alex Cox has appeared in various films including *Backtrack* (1989, directed by Dennis Hopper) as DH Lawrence, *Floundering* (1994, directed by Peter McCarthy) as the Photographer, *Dead Beat* (1994, directed by Adam Dubov) as the English Teacher, *La Reina de la Noche* (1994, directed by Arturo Ripstein) as Klaus Eder, *Perdita Durango* (1997, directed by Alex de la Iglesia) as Agent Doyle, *La Ley de Herodes* (1998, directed by Luis Estrada) and, most recently, *Gimmie Power* (1999, directed by Fernando Sarinana).

The films on the following pages are those that Alex Cox wrote and/or directed.

SLEEP IS FOR SISSIES aka EDGE CITY

(USA, 1980, 40 min)

Production company: Commies From Mars Corporation
Director: Alex Cox
Photography: Michael Miner
Music: Gregg Weissman
Second Unit Director: Nancy King
Additional Photography: Tom Richmond, Lou Weinberg and Nancy King
Production Manager: David Burton
Sound: Dan Halperin
Assistant Camera: Prudence Faxon, David Boyd and Rose-Marie Turko
Cast: Alex Cox (Roy Rawlings), Bob Rosen (Smack Hasty), with Christine Burton, Bill Wood, Apache Rodriguez, RL Benjamin, Shaun Madigan and Greg Alarcon

SCARRED

(USA, 1984, 85 min)

Production company: Seymour Borde
Director: Marie Turko
Assistant Director: Alex Cox
Producers: Marie Turko, Mark Borde and Dan Halperin
Executive Producer: Seymour Borde
Screenplay: Marie Turko
Photography: Michael Miner
Editor: Marie Turko
Art Director: Cecilia Rodarte
Cast: Jennifer Mayo (Ruby Star), Jackie Berryman (Carla), David Dean (Easy), Rico L Richardson (Jojo) and Debra Dion (Sandy)

REPO MAN

(USA, 1984, 94 min)

Production company: Edge City / Released by Universal
Director: Alex Cox
Producers: Jonathan Wacks and Peter McCarthy
Executive Producer: Michael Nesmith
Associate Producer: Gerald Olson
Screenplay: Alex Cox
Photography: Robby Muller
Editor: Dennis Dolan
Music: Steven Hufsteter, Tito Larriva, Iggy Pop (*Repo Man* theme)
Art Director: J Rae Fox and Lynda Burbank
Cast: Harry Dean Stanton (Bud), Emilio Estevez (Otto), Tracey Walter (Miller), Olivia Barash (Leila), Sy Richardson (Lite), Susan Barnes (Agent Rogers), Fox Harris (J Frank Parnell), Tom Finnegan (Oly), Del Zamora (Lagarto), Eddie Velez (Napo), Zander Schloss (Kevin), Jennifer Balgobin (Debbi), Dick Rude (Duke), Miguel Sandoval (Archie), Vonetta McGee (Marlene)

SID AND NANCY

(UK/USA, 1985, 111 min)

Production company: Zenith / Initial
Director: Alex Cox
Producer: Eric Fellner
Co-Producer: Peter McCarthy
Associate Producer: Peter Jacques and Abbe Wool
Screenplay: Alex Cox and Abbe Wool
Photography: Roger Deakins
Editor: David Martin
Music: The Pogues, Pray for Rain and Joe Strummer
Production Design: Linda Burbank, J Rae Fox and Andrew McAlpine
Cast: Gary Oldman (Sid Vicious), Chloe Webb (Nancy Spungen), David Hayman (Malcolm McLaren), Debby Bishop (Phoebe), Drew Schofield (Johnny Rotten), Xander Berkeley (Bowery Snax), Perry Benson (Paul), Tony London (Steve), Sandy Baron (Hotelier USA), Sy Richardson (Methadone Caseworker), Edward Tudor Pole (Hotelier UK) Biff Yeager (Detective), Courtney Love (Gretchen), Kathy Burke (Brenda)

STRAIGHT TO HELL

(UK/Spain, 1986, 86 min)

Production company: Initial / Released by Island
Director: Alex Cox
Producer: Eric Fellner
Executive Producers: Cary Brokaw and Scott Millaney
Associate Producer: Paul Raphael
Screenplay: Alex Cox and Dick Rude
Photography: Tom Richmond
Editor: David Martin
Music: The Pogues and Pray for Rain
Production Design: Andrew McAlpine
Art Director: Caroline Hanania
Cast: Sy Richardson (Norwood), Dick Rude (Willy), Courtney Love (Velma), Joe Strummer (Simms), Zander Schloss (Karl), Del Zamora (Poncho), Luis Contreras (Sal), Jim Jarmusch (Mr Amos Dade), Miguel Sandoval (George), Jennifer Balgobin (Fabienne), Biff Yeager (Frank), Sue Kiel (Leticia), Michele Winstanley (Louise), Xander Berkeley (Preacher), Fox Harris (Kim Blousson), Dennis Hopper (IG Farben), Grace Jones (Sonya), Kathy Burke (Sabrina), Elvis Costello (Hives), The Pogues (The MacMahons), Sara Sugarman (Chuch)

WALKER

(USA/Nicaragua, 1987, 95 min)

Production company: Edward R Pressman; Incine / Released by Northern Distribution Partners; Universal
Director: Alex Cox
Producers: Lorenzo O'Brien and Angel Flores Marini
Executive Producer: Edward R Pressman
Associate Producer: Debbie Diaz
Screenplay: Rudy Wurlitzer
Photography: David Bridges
Editors: Carlos Puente and Alex Cox
Music: Joe Strummer
Production Design: Bruno Rubeo
Art Director: Cecilia Montiel and Jorge Sainz
Cast: Ed Harris (William Walker), Richard Masur (Ephraim Squier), Rene Auberjonois (Ma Siegfried Henningson), Keith Szarabajka (Timothy Crocker), Sy Richardson (Captain Hornsby), Xander Berkeley (Bryon Cole), John Diehl (Stebbins), Peter Boyle (Cornelius Vanderbilt), Marlee Matlin (Ellen Martin), Alfonso Arau (Raousset), Pedro Armendariz Jr (Munoz), Roberto Lopez Espinoza (Mayorga), Blanca Guerra (Yrena), Miguel Sandoval (Parker French) and Joe Strummer (Faucet)

EL PATRULLERO (HIGHWAY PATROLMAN)

(Mexico/Japan, 1991, 104 min)

Production company: Cable Hogue Company; Marubeni; Together Brothers; Ultra Films / Released by First Look Pictures

Director: Alex Cox

Producer: Lorenzo O'Brien

Co-Producer: Jean Michel Lacor

Executive Producer: Sammy O Masada and Kuniaki Negishi

Associate Producer: Brant Reiter

Screenplay: Lorenzo O'Brien

Photography: Miguel Garzon

Editor: Carlos Puente

Music: Zander Schloss

Production Design: Cecilia Montiel

Cast: Roberto Sosa (Pedro), Bruno Bichir (Anibal), Vanessa Bauche (Maribel), Zaide Silvia Gutierrez (Griselda), Pedro Armendariz Jr (Sergeant Barreras), Malena Doria (Abuela), Towi Islas (Emilio), Ernesto Gomez Cruz (Commander Navarro), Mike Moroff (Commander Sanchez), Jorge Russek (Mr Mateos) Ana Bertha Espin (Mrs. Sanchez), Eduardo Lopez Rojas (Mr Roja)

THE WINNER

(USA, 1996, 90 min)

Production company: MDP Worldwide / Released by LIVE Entertainment

Director: Alex Cox

Producer: Kenneth Schwenker

Co-Producer: Wendy Riss and Jeremiah Samuels

Executive Producers: Mark Damon and Rebecca DeMornay

Screenplay: Wendy Riss

Photography: Denis Maloney

Editor: Carlos Puente

Original Music: Pray for Rain and Zander Schloss

Production Design: Cecilia Montiel

Cast: Rebecca DeMornay (Louise), Vincent D'Onofrio (Philip), Frank Whaley (Joey), Delroy Lindo (Kingman), Michael Madsen (Wolf), Billy Bob Thornton (Jack), Richard Edson (Frankie), Saverio Guerra (Paulie)

DEATH AND THE COMPASS

(UK/Japan/Mexico, 1996, 90 min)

Production company: PSC; KHB; Together Brothers; Cable Hogue
Director: Alex Cox
Producers: Lorenzo O'Brien and Karl H Braun
Executive Producer: Katsumi Ishikuma
Associate Producer: Kuniaki Negishi
Screenplay: Alex Cox (based on the story by Jorge Luis Borges)
Photography: Miguel Garzon
Editor: Carlos Puente
Music: Pray for Rain
Production Design: Cecilia Montiel
Cast: Peter Boyle (Lonnrot), Miguel Sandoval (Treviranus), Christopher Ecclestone (Zunz), Zaide Silvia Gutierrez (Ms Espinoza), Pedro Armendariz Jr (Blot), Alonso Echanove (Novalis), Eduardo Lopez Rojas (Black Finnegan), Arianne Pellicer (Natasha), Gabriela Gurrola (Hooker), Rene Pereyra (Azevedo), Mario Ivan Martinez (Hotel Manager), Roberto Sosa (Drug Addict 1), Bruno Bichir (Drug Addict 2), Abel Woolrich (Barman), Martin LaSalle (Dr Yarmolinsky), Luis de Icaza (Bigot), Claudio Brook (Narrator), Karl Braun (Sergeant), Alex Cox (Commander Borges)

FEAR AND LOATHING IN LAS VEGAS

(USA, 1998, 128 min)

Production company: Rhino Films / Released by Universal
Director: Terry Gilliam
Producers: Laila Nablusi, Patrick Cassavetti, Steve Nemeth
Co-Producer: Elliot Lewis Rosenblatt
Executive Producers: Harold Bronson and Richard Foos
Screenplay: Tod Davies, Alex Cox, Terry Gilliam and Tony Grissoni (from the book by Hunter S Thompson)
Photography: Nicola Percorini
Editor: Leslie Walker
Production Design: Alex McDowell
Art Directors: Gary Diamond and Chris Gorak
Cast: Johnny Depp (Raoul Duke), Benicio Del Toro (Dr Gonzo), Tobey Maguire (Hitch-hiker), Ellen Barkin (North Star Waitress), Gary Busey (Highway Patrolman), Christina Ricci (Lucy), Mark Harmon (Lacerda), Cameron Diaz (Blonde TV Reporter), Lyle Lovett (Musician), Flea (Musician), Harry Dean Stanton (Judge)

THREE BUSINESSMEN

(Netherlands / USA / Japan, 1998, 83 min)

Production company: Exterminating Angel
Director: Alex Cox
Producer: Tod Davies
Executive Producer: Wim Kayzer
Associate Producer: Katsumi Ishikuma
Screenplay: Tod Davies
Photography: Robert Tregenza
Editor: Alex Cox
Music: Pray For Rain (title song performed by Debbie Harry)
Sound Design: Richard Beggs
Special Visual Effects: Rocco Gioffre
Cast: Miguel Sandoval (Bennie), Robert Wisdom (Leroy), Alex Cox (Frank), Isabel Ampudia (Josefina), Andrew Schofield (Desk Clerk), Adrian Kai (Maitre D'), John McMartin (Liverpool Businessman), Christine Colvin (Liverpool Barmaid), Adrian Henri (Poet), Tomorowo Taguchi (Noodle Shop Man), Ryoko Takizawa (Noodle Shop Woman), Masatoshi Nagase (Blind Man)